WILLIAM HARPER

SERGIO BUSTAMANTE

LAURINDA SPEAR

ANDY WARHOL

ELSA PERETTI

FRITZ SCHOLDER

ROBERT HEINDEL

MASSIMO VIGNELLI

D0461737

JAMES ROSENQUIST

NANCY GRAVES

PHILIPPE STARCK

(PH.S)

LOIS GREENFIELD

RICHARD HAAS

CHRISTO/JEANNE CLAUDE

ALLAN HOUSER

BJØRN WIINBLAD

ERNEST TROVA

MARK MILLER

MICHAEL GRAVES

FAY JONES

LINCOLN FOX

BOŘEK ŠÍPEK

ALEXANDER CALDER

RICHARD MEIER

CESAR PELLI

DOUGLAS KIRKLAND

MANZU

NORMAN FOSTER

MICHAEL PARKES

HILTON MCCONNICO

DEAN FEARING

ZANDRA RHODES

JAMES WINES

BON PAINTER

ROBERT VENTURI

ANTOINE PREDOCK

CUISINE of the CREATIVE

A COOKBOOK by JAMES LAMBETH and MILES JAMES

MIAMI DOG PRESS, JOHNSON, AR, USA

Copyright 1998 © MIAMI DOG PRESS, INCORPORATED All rights reserved. No part of this book may be reproduced in any form except for reviews, without the written permission of the publisher.

MIAMI DOG PRESS, INC,
3906 Greathouse Springs Road, Post Office Box 409, Johnson, Arkansas 72741
Tel. 501-521-1304/Toll Free 888-289-7090, Fax.501-521-8091, MIAMIDOG @AOL.COM

Book design and food photography by James Lambeth, FAIA, FAAR
Food design, preparation and selected recipes by Chef Miles James
Computer Graphics and Typography by Wendy Lott, Bella Vista, AR

GRATEFUL ACKNOWLEDGEMENT IS MADE FOR PERMISSION TO USE THE FOLLOWING:
Photograph of James Rosenquist, p 4 by Jim McHugh for TYLER GRAPHICS LTD. • Photograph of Antoine Predock, p 5 by © Robert Reck, 1986 • © 1998 Artists Rights Society (ARS), New York/ADAGP, Paris pp 18-21 • "Wrapped Reichstag, Berlin 1971-1995," © Christo/Jeanne Claude, Photograph © Wolfgang Voltz, pp 22, 24, "Surrounded Islands, Biscayne Bay, Greater Miami, 1983" © Christo/Jeanne Claude, Photograph © Wolfgang Voltz, p 23 • Recipes from COOKING WITH DAVID BURKE by David Burke and Carmel Berman Reingold (Alfred A. Knopf, NYC, 1995, pp 12, 13) by permission of David Burke • © 1998 Demart Pro Arte (R), Geneva/Artists Rights Society (ARS), New York pp 26-29 • By permission The Swan/Dolphin Walt Disney World Resorts®, p 43 • © Richard Haas/Licensed by VAGA, New York, N.Y., pp 54-57 • Quote from WOMEN OF THE APACHE NATION.. VOICES OF TRUTH by H. Henrietta Stockel, © 1991 By The University of Nevada Press, reprinted with permission of The University of Nevada Press, pp 72-73 • © Elsa Peretti Designs, exclusively for Tiffany & Co., pp 91, 131, 134-137 • Recipes from THE COYOTE CAFE © 1989 Mark Miller, (Ten Speed Press, Berkley, CA), pp 112, 113, by permission of Mark Miller • Recipes from DEAN FEARING'S SOUTHWEST CUISINE © 1990 by Rosewood Property Company (Grove Weidenfeld Press, NYC), by permission of Dean Fearing, pp 32-33, 226 • © Nancy Graves Foundation/Licensed by VAGA, New York, NY. pp 46-49 • Murals © Richard Haas/Licensed by VAGA, New York, NY. pp 54-56 • Recipes from THE WOLFGANG PUCK COOK BOOK © 1986 Wolfgang Puck (Random House, NY), pp 148-149, 228 • Recipe from pp 53 "Pecan Cashew Glazed Swordfish by permission of D. Brewley and M. Caracciolo • Photographs © Lois Greenfield, pp 50, 51, 52 • "Best Buddies"© and "Andy Mouse"© 1985 the Estate of Keith Haring pp 88-91 • "Marilyn Monroe" Photograph © Douglas Kirkland pp 82-84 • Photograph p 114 by Miles James • © Roy Lichtenstein Estate, 1998, pp 90-93 •"Swan Spirit," "The Juggler," and " Angel of Dawn" © 1994 Michael Parkes, pp 122-124, courtesy: Steltman Gallery and Editions, Amsterdam, the Netherlands • Photograph p 130 by Tiffany Larimer • Recipe courtesy "The Shed" Santa Fe, NM, p 141 • Photographs of Zandra Rhodes by Robyn Beeche pp 158, 161 • Art © James Rosenquist/Licensed by VAGA, New York, NY. pp 168-171 • "Onion," "Mushroom," and "Banana," © 1996 Fritz Scholder pp 172-177 • "Felix" photographs by permission of the Peninsula Hotel, Hong Kong, pp 188-189 • "Flowers" © and "Self Portrait," © The Andy Warhol Foundation for the Visual Arts/ARS, New York pp 210-212 • "Highway 86," © 1986 James Wines, "Street Glass Necklace," ©1994 Kriz Kizak, p 218 • "Imperial" and "Cabaret" Dinnerware by Tiffany & Co. Copyrighted designs owned by the Frank Lloyd Wright Foundation, pp 67, 222-223

A portion of the royalties from this book is being donated to The American Academy in Rome (JL)
A portion of the royalties from this book is being donated to The James Beard Foundation, NY (MJ)

LIBRARY OF CONGRESS CATALOGUING-IN-PUBLICATION DATA

Lambeth, James, 1942-
Cuisine of the creative: a cookbook/by James Lambeth and Miles James. -- 1st ed.
p. cm.
Includes bibliographical references and index.
ISBN 0-9601678-3-8 (alk. paper). -- ISBN 0-9601678-4-6 (pbk. : alk. paper)
1. Cookery. 2. Artists -- Biography. 3. Architects -- Biography. 4. Cooks -- Biography. I.James, Miles, 1968- . II. Title.
TX714.L338 1998   97-49870
641.5--dc21   CIP

Printed in Canada by D.W. Friesens, Printers through Four Color Imports, Ltd. First Edition 1998 ISBN 0-9601678.3.8 (HB) ISBN 0-9601678.4.6 (PB)

PHILIPPE STARCK'S "GLASS OBJECT WITH PAINTED RESIN APPLE" FOR THE PREMIERE OF THE PENINSULA HOTEL TOWER, HONG KONG, DECEMBER 1, 1994

DEDICATED TO
DALE HUSMANN
MARTIN TALBOT
NANCY GRAVES
ALLAN HOUSER
ROY LICHTENSTEIN

3

TABLE OF CONTENTS

JAMES ROSENQUIST AND COURTNEY AT HIS MUSEUM OF MODERN ART OPENING, NEW YORK

MILES, COURTNEY AND MARK MILLER AT HIS RED SAGE RESTAURANT, WASHINGTON, DC

COURTNEY, ZANDRA RHODES, JOYCE, AND JIM AT "DYNASEN GALLERY," NEW ORLEANS, LA

NANCY GRAVES, JOHN D'ARMS AND MANZÚ AT AN AMERICAN ACADEMY IN ROME OPENING

DR JONAS SALK AND SIR NORMAN FOSTER
AIA GOLD MEDAL CEREMONY, LOS ANGELES

JOYCE WITH ROY LICHTENSTEIN AT CASTELLI
PARTY FOR JAMES ROSENQUIST, NEW YORK

COURTNEY AND MICHAEL GRAVES, AT THE
UNITED STATES AMBASSADOR'S RES., ROME

ANTOINE PREDOCK AT HIS ARCHITECTURAL
STUDIO IN ALBUQUERQUE, NEW MEXICO

We shot through L.A. like a a ricocheting bullet. The opulence and violence of this schizophrenic city became a blur as we sped eastward into the aubergine twilight of the Mojave Desert. Joyce and I had flown into LAX that morning to take delivery of a new Speedster and were adventuring homeward, first to Las Vegas, then to Santa Fe, and finally to the Ozark Mountains.

As the quiet of the desert began to surround us, we discovered the "new car" had no radio... no electric opiate to fill the void of the night. The awkward silence soon became unbearable -- slowly, we began an epic three day conversation.

We talked about the lunch we had that afternoon at Granita in Malibu and about the beautiful food, the beautiful design, the breeding habits of celebrities, and the inflated egos of mâitre d's.

We discussed our favorite foods and the favorite dishes of the many artists and architects we had met in the past. We began to wonder about the connection between food and creativity. Did "What you eat, you are," apply to the elusive creative spirit? An idea began to form that would engage us for the next four years.

Our daughter, Courtney, had just gotten engaged to Chef Miles James. The possibility of doing a project with him would introduce us to his mastery of the culinary arts as well as involve him in our world of art and architecture. Miles could create the food, and I could photograph it. We could explore the connection between food and creativity together. CUISINE OF THE CREATIVE was born.

Our list of "creative favorites" would eventually include over fifty of the world's most influential artists, architects, photographers and chefs. They were the "fountainheads" who inspired our taste, our fashion, and our aesthetic environment. The force of their personalities had created and led entire movements in the arts. They would form the structure of our idea conceived in the silence of the Mojave Desert.

On spring break from the university in '62, I met Salvador Dali and his wife Gala at a party in Manhattan. I had been invited by a classmate's parents. (Broadway producers Fred and Joyce Coe). Dali was embracing Gala in one hand and his gold knobbed cane in the other. "I love ingesting suits of arms. I especially love the mystical crayfish." He went on to say, "If I hate that detestable vegetable spinach, it is because it is shapeless, like Liberty!" For Dali, Miles created a wonderful crayfish consommè recipe.

Courtney, while on a weekend break from Vassar in '87, met both Andy Warhol and Keith Haring in Saks Fifth Avenue. During their brief and terrifying conversation, Haring said he lived on "Street Food," and Warhol said he preferred "fish and watermelon," because they were so slimming. On that dazzling Saturday afternoon, she walked away with a copy of Warhol's "Interview" (The one with Cybil Shephard on the cover), and a "Keith Haring Swatch Watch," both autographed. In '95, James Rosenquist invited us to a party after his Castelli Gallery opening in Soho. The icons of Pop Art were there. Joyce met Roy Lichtenstein, and he admitted he loved "Broccoli Rabe" and tried to eat it everyday. I built up my courage and approached Claes Oldenburg who was talking with Leo Castelli in the corner. I was politely greeted, and when I finally asked about their favorite food, Oldenburg smiled and said he preferred it "stuffed!" Another curious response included architect Frank Gehry, whose dazzling Guggenheim Museum in Bilbao, Spain, was just completed, wrote,"I don't have a favorite food or recipe that I am engulfed with. I don't know anything about cooking. It is just not my thing. When you get into ice skating, let me know."

JOYCE AND HILTON MC CONNICO IN HIS SECRET FLOWER GARDEN, PARIS, FRANCE

JOYCE, ZANDRA RHODES, AND COURTNEY IN ZANDRA'S LONDON TOWNHOUSE LIVING ROOM

ERNEST TROVA AND JOYCE AT HIS OPENING PARTY, PHILIP SAMUELS GALLERY, ST. LOUIS

COURTNEY, BJØRN WIINBLAD, AND JOYCE AT "WIINBLAD HAUS" OPENING, DALLAS,TX

Frederic Remington shared Salvador Dali's disgust for the green stuff. He hated spinach. He also hated Virginia ham because it "tasted like stove logs." On the other hand Remington loved what he called a "Cavalry Breakfast," a cigarette and a shot of whiskey. James Rosenquist, to ward off hunger, suggested "three fingers of whiskey." Andy Warhol controlled his weight with his 'New York City Diet,' "When I order in a restaurant, I order everything that I don't want, so I have a lot to play around with while everyone else eats." Frank Lloyd Wright and Sarah Bernhardt used the same philosophy of dieting. They ate what they wanted when they wanted it, but never, never ate all they wanted. They always left food on their plate no matter how hungry they were. They remained slender and lived to be very old indeed.

Our choice of artists covered a wide social spectrum. Philippe Starck "the 'Rock Star' in the world of design," did a wonderful "recipe drawing" for us of the simplest and most elegant of foods. On the other hand, Bon Painter "an obscure artist savant" was the town drunk of the small country village of Watts, Oklahoma. He terrorized the citizens with his critical paintings of their social behavior. His food, like his art, was primitive, bizarre, and delicious.

Some of the artists were less adventuresome when it came to new food. Allan Houser, one of America's greatest sculptors, was raised on a farm in Apache, Oklahoma, where,"meat was cooked until it was definitely dead, and potatoes boiled to tastelessness." Italian sculptor Manzu said, "I am a peasant. I eat peasant food."

Some of the artists had more rarified tastes. New Yorker/Arkansan architect Edward Durrell Stone said he loved his food, "out of season, underage, under glass or on fire." When he traveled home to the Ozarks, his favorite cuisine was 'southern fried chicken and black

eyed peas.' Another "AIA Gold Medal" winning Ozark architect, Fay Jones, has long been known for his culinary escapades. He once told me he "enjoyed six meals one day in New Orleans." This led to his nickname Buf-Fay Jones.

Richard Meier, one of our most elegant architects, just completed the Getty Museum (The World's Richest Museum) on a hilltop in Los Angeles. To our surprise, his food of choice was a wonderful "down home" recipe for Bar-B-Que Chicken using Coca-Cola® in the sauce.

If there was a favorite food among our artists, it was Italian. With names like Pucci, Vignelli, Manzu, Trova , Venturi, and Peretti, this wasn't surprising; but also names like Graves, Foster, Heindel, and Jones preferred Italian dishes. James Rosenquist told me, " one evening I cooked pasta in my village studio for Michael Douglas and three queens: the Queen of Denmark, the Queen of Norway, and the Queen of Sweden."

Our Porsche is now four years old, and Courtney and Miles just celebrated their third wedding anniversary. They created a world class restaurant "James at the Mill," and live in one of my early designs. The CUISINE OF THE CREATIVE was a long and exciting journey that led us around the world to prepare and photograph its exquisite foods.

We hope you find the recipes as rich and wonderful as we do, and that you use them often. We also hope that the foods will evoke memories of the art and architecture as well as the artists and architects who created them. Do enjoy the ride!

J.L.
Bora Bora, French Polynesia
December 1997

COURTNEY AND JAMES ROSENQUIST, AT HER PORTRAIT SITTING, ARIPEKA, FLORIDA

MILES, LAURINDA SPEAR, AND COURTNEY AT ARQUITECTONICA STUDIO, MIAMI, FLORIDA

JOYCE, COURTNEY, AND ALLAN HOUSER AT THE MUSEUM OF ART, SANTA FE, NEW MEXICO

FRITZ SCHOLDER AND JOYCE AT THE SENA GALLERY OPENING, SANTA FE, NEW MEXICO

6:00 a.m. Miami, Florida. It was partly cloudy as the sun came up over a glistening Biscayne Bay. The city still slept except for the few making their way home from the previous last night parties. Jim and I awoke at 5:30 to gather food ingredients, film, batteries, slave flashes, and all the the necessary props for the first of many photo shoots to come. We made our way up to the red spiral staircase that cantilevers above the twelve mirrored stories below. The yellow, red, and blue of the "Atlantis Skycourt" that has come to be known as one of the defining elements of the Miami skyline would pair wonderfully with the rich colors of Laurinda Spear's "Miami Paella." Like two crazed hang-gliders, we perched ourselves on a rickety table high above the top ledge of the staircase and waited for the clouds to drift away. The sun popped through, and yielded the perfect light. We shot at least sixty shots. Jim always said," Film is cheap; Location is not." The brilliant stone crab claws, yellow rice and blue mussels looked beautiful hanging above the bubbling hot tub below. The first shot was a success!

A few months later on a hot and steamy Saturday morning, we found ourselves in Atlanta, home of Coca-Cola® and Richard Meier's High Museum of Art. After months of faxing, letter writing, and phone calls we arrived with recipes and food in tow. We started to set up on the front lawn to shoot Mr. Meier's Coca-Cola® BBQ Chicken and watermelon. Immediately, three guards came rushing out to greet us and politely told us to "keep off the grass." We chose to shoot from the sidewalk. The biggest challenge was keeping the flock of street people, still intoxicated from the night before, from snatching the food. After several interesting conversations with former lawyers, former accountants, and current porn pushers, we successfully captured the shot and gave the street dwellers a great southern breakfast.

9:00 a.m. Hong Kong. Time had run out. We had been waiting for the fog to lift for three days. From our room on the twenty-fifth floor of the Ritz Carlton, we could barely see I.M. Pei's exquisite Bank of China and Sir Norman Foster's hi-tech Bank of Hong Kong. As we were packing to leave, the fog slowly began to lift. In a frenzy, we grabbed the food, loaded the camera, and got the shots. Later, as we were sitting on the Kai Tak runway on our flight to Bangkok, we could see the stunning skyline across Hong Kong Harbor, shimmering in a crystal clear sky.

January, Beaver Lake, Arkansas. Great clouds of hot breath charged from the moist nose of the one ton beast they call Cody. Crouching in the snow-covered field, I carefully place Fritz Scholder's chile on a Navajo "American Flag" horse blanket. As Fritz said, "It evokes fond memories of woods." In the distance, Cody's relatives and descendants stared with quizzical looks on their huge, icy, buffalo faces. Bunky Boger, the ex-rodeo clown and proud owner of "the most traveled and photographed buffalo in America" (one of Richard Avedon's favorites), had just taken us through his ranch of mountain lions, bobcats, miniature horses and other strange and wild creatures. A perfect setting for Fritz Scholder's southwest chile.

For me, CUISINE OF THE CREATIVE has been a wonderful way to get to know some of the world's most creative people. Through all of the correspondence, food preparation, photo shoots, and travels abroad, it has been the richest experience of my professional life. We have chosen the artists that we admire the most. I hope some or all of the artists become your favorites too. In every photograph, we have attempted to illustrate the food as a complement to the art. In some ways, I think the recipes have given a personal and unique perspective of the art and of the artists. I have found great inspiration through all of the artists, architects, designers, chefs and photographers involved in this book. I hope you, too, are inspired by CUISINE OF THE CREATIVE.

M.J.
Lanai, Hawaii
January, 1998

WILLIAM HARPER AND MILES IN THE HARPER CLOISONNÉ STUDIO IN TALLAHASSEE, FLORIDA

CESAR PELLI AND COURTNEY AT AIA GOLD MEDAL CEREMONY, LOS ANGELES, CALIFORNIA

MICHAEL PARKES IN HIS STUDIO, SPAIN

DAVID BURKE AND MILES IN ASPEN, COLORADO

R E C I P E S Y M B O L S

○

FOOD CHOICE FROM INTERVIEW:
RECIPE FROM ARTIST

△

FOOD CHOICE FROM INTERVIEW:
RECIPE FROM CHEF MILES JAMES

◇

FOOD CHOICE FROM INTERVIEW:
RECIPE FROM OTHERS

▢

FOOD CHOICE FROM RESEARCH:
RECIPE FROM CHEF MILES JAMES

▽

TO COMPLEMENT ARTISTS' FOODS:
RECIPE FROM CHEF MILES JAMES

> Chef Miles James'
> Recommended Beverages

ROBERT HEINDEL IN HIS 300-YEAR OLD FARM
HOUSE PAINTING STUDIO, IN EASTON, CT

PHILIPPE STARCK CHAIR IN "FELIX" RESTAURANT
THE PENINSULA HOTEL, HONG KONG, CHINA

LINCOLN FOX IN HIS STUDIO IN PAONIA,
COLORADO, "SHAMAN WITH BEAR SKULL"

COURTNEY AND DEAN FEARING, "THE MANSION
ON TURTLE CREEK RESTAURANT," DALLAS, TEXAS

"My philosophy on food and cooking has changed many times and continues to change somewhat as I continue to learn. But, I always follow my instinct with my craft, trying always to work with the highest quality people and products and making sure each dish tastes good and satisfies."

1962	b. Hazlet, New Jersey.
1979	Decided to become chef while working with Miriam Brickman. This year he met Paula Wolfert, Marcella Hazan, John Clancy and Henry Hugh.
1980	Broiler chef at Navesink Country Club, NJ.
1983	Graduated from the Culinary Institute of America in Hyde Park, NY.
1983	Worked in Fredrikstad, Norway at a small inn for the Stolt-Nielsen family.
1984	Became saucier at "La Crèmaillière" in Banksville, NY.
1986	Traveled to France and joined Michel Fourreau, at LaRapiere in Mauvezin.
1986	Returned to U.S. and worked for Daniel Boulud at the Hotel Plaza Athènèe in New York City, became sous-chef at the River Cafe in Brooklyn, NY. for Charlie Palmer.
1987	Returned to France for more experience with classic technique studying at Chez la Mère Blanc in Vonnas, then to L'Espèrance in Vèzelay, Burgundy. Later he took classes at Maison Blanche and worked with Marc Meneau, the Troisgros brothers' and Gaston Lenòtre and became executive chef at the River Cafe.
1988	First American Chef to receive Meilleurs Ouviers de France medal and diploma. Won Nippon Award of Excellence in Tokyo, Japan.
1990	Opened Park Avenue Cafe in NY, co-owner with Allan Stillman.
1991	Voted "Chef of the Year" by his American peers.
1995	"COOKING WITH DAVID BURKE" with Carmel Broman Reingold, (Knopf, NY).
1996	Introduced food line "Pastrami Salmon™". Opened "Park Avenue Cafe," Chicago.
1998	Lives in New York City.

. . . .

PARFAIT OF SALMON AND TUNA TARTARS WITH CRÈMÉ FRAÎCHE
serves 10

To form the parfait, you will need cylindrical rings that are approximately two inches high and two inches in diameter.

When I devised this dish, I went to a hardware store that specialized in construction material and had them cut steel pipes into two-inch rings. However, any circular object can be used: pastry rings, cookie cutters, biscuit cutters, pancake rings, and even bracelets.

The parfait can also be prepared in a ramekin or demitasse cup, but then the impact of viewing the parfait in its entirety is lost.

1 cup crème fraîche
2 shallots, peeled and minced
4 tablespoons olive oil
2 tablespoons chopped capers
2 teaspoons lemon zest
4 teaspoons soy sauce
2 teaspoons ground horseradish
2 tablespoons chopped coriander
2 tablespoons chopped chervil
10 ounces yellowfin tuna, diced
10 ounces salmon, ground
2 teaspoons coarse or kosher salt
2 teaspoons freshly ground pepper
olive oil for rings
10 ounces Osetra or other caviar (optional)*

*If you wish, you may spoon 2 tablespoons of caviar on top of salmon mixture before topping with crème fraiche. You will then have 4 layers.

Whip crème fraîche until thick, and stiff peaks are formed. Reserve in refrigerator.

Combine shallots and olive oil in a small saucepan and sautè until shallots are translucent. Place shallots in a bowl and add capers, lemon zest, soy sauce, horseradish, coriander, and chervil. Mix until combined. Divide shallot mixture into two equal parts. Combine one

PREVIOUS TWO PAGES: FIRST, "PARFAIT OF SALMON AND TUNA TARTARS" SECOND: "WILD MUSHROOM FLAN WITH SHRIMP" half with diced tuna; combine the other half with ground salmon. Add 1 teaspoon salt and 1 teaspoon pepper to the tuna mixture and mix until all ingredients are combined. Add 1 teaspoon salt and 1 teaspoon pepper to salmon mixture and mix until all ingredients are combined. Lightly brush inside of 10 rings or molds with olive oil. Place waxed paper on a cookie sheet. Place molds on the cookie sheet.

To Assemble:
Place 2 tablespoons of tuna mixture in each mold. Smooth tuna mixture with back of spoon. Place 2 tablespoons of salmon mixture on top of tuna mixture. Smooth salmon mixture with back of spoon. Add 2 tablespoons of crème fraîche. Smooth with blade of flat knife, making sure that crème fraîche is level with top of mold. You should have 3 equal levels.

Chill in refrigerator for 2 to 3 hours. Place each ring or mold on a plate and gently remove mold, leaving parfait on plate. Serve with toast.

STEAK DIANE WITH WILD-MUSHROOM FLAN

(Flan may be served as an appetizer only)
serves 4

2 tablespoons clarified butter

1/2 pound wild mushrooms
(chanterelle, shiitake, morel), finely minced

---

1 cup heavy sweet cream

---

2 eggs, lightly beaten

---

coarse or kosher salt
and freshly ground pepper

---

1 tablespoon chopped foie gras
(optional)

Preheat oven to 350°F. Heat butter in a large saucepan. Add mushrooms and cook, stirring, for 2 minutes. Stir in heavy cream and slowly whip in eggs and egg yolk. Season to taste. Strain. Pour flan mixture into 4 ramekins (or 4 eggshells), add truffle and foie gras, if you wish, and place in a bain-marie (water bath).

Cover each ramekin with foil and bake for 25 minutes, or until flan is set and a skewer piercing side of flan comes out clean. Prepare

steaks and sauce while flans bake.

4 strip steaks, about 5 to 5 1/2
ounces each

---

coarse or kosher salt and
freshly ground pepper to taste

---

4 tablespoons clarified butter
or olive oil

---

1 shallot, minced

1/2 pound chanterelle
mushrooms, sliced
(white mushrooms may be used)

---

4 tablespoons red wine

---

4 tablespoons red-wine vinegar

---

1 tablespoon cracked
peppercorns

---

1 1/2 cups brown stock
or dark chicken stock
or canned beef broth

---

1 tablespoon chopped
fresh tarragon
or 1 teaspoon dried tarragon

---

4 tablespoons butter

---

2 tablespoons whole-grain mustard

---

1 tablespoon dijon mustard

Season steaks with salt and pepper. Heat clarified butter or olive oil in a large sauté pan. Add steaks to pan and sauté for about 3 to 5 minutes on each side, turning, until both sides are nicely browned. Remove steaks from pan and keep warm. Drain all but 1 tablespoon of fat from pan. Add shallot and mushrooms, sauté for 1 minute, stirring. Add red wine, red-wine vinegar, peppercorns and cook over high heat, stirring, until all but 1 tablespoon of liquid has evaporated.

Add brown stock, dark chicken stock or broth and reduce by half. Stir in tarragon, salt, and pepper. Whisk in butter and add both mustards. Continue cooking, over low heat, until sauce has thickened slightly.

Remove from heat.

To build this dish:
Carve each steak into thin slices. Turn a wild-mushroom flan into the center of each of 4 dinner plates, and fan meat around flan. Spoon over sauce.

Variation: This dish may also be prepared with venison loin steaks.

Stag's Leap Wine Cellars Cabernet Sauvignon, 1995, Napa Valley, California

COCONUT TRUFFLES
serves 4

2 cups heavy sweet cream

3/4 cup grated coconut

---

1 1/2 pounds white chocolate,
finely chopped

---

4 ounces butter, slightly softened

---

1 pound bittersweet chocolate,
melted

Combine cream and coconut in a saucepan and bring to a boil. Allow to steep for 30 minutes and strain. Bring to a second boil. Place white chocolate in a bowl and add hot cream mixture to chocolate. Beat until chocolate has melted and all ingredients are combined. Add butter gradually and continue beating. Chill mixture and form into cherry-sized balls. Dip each ball into melted chocolate. Place truffles in paper candy cups or into a parchment- or waxed-paper-lined box.

CHOCOLATE TRUFFLES WITH COFFEE FLAVOR
yeild 30

2 cups heavy sweet cream

---

4 tablespoons finely ground coffee
(not instant)

1/2 pound bittersweet chocolate,
finely chopped

---

4 tablespoons butter,
slightly softened

---

unsweetened cocoa powder

Combine cream and coffee in a saucepan and bring to a boil. Allow to steep for 30 minutes and bring to a second boil. Place chocolate in a bowl, add hot cream mixture and all ingredients are combined.

Add butter gradually and continue beating. Chill mixture and form into balls. Roll truffles in cocoa and place in paper candy cups or into a parchment or waxed-paper-lined box.

"My earliest recollections are a blend of folklore, dreams and reality: pots of gold hidden in hollow trees, the curl of pipe-smoke as my grandfather told stories of his boyhood in China, stars that fell to the beach at night and waited for the pure of heart."

1943	b. Culiacan, Mexico of Chinese/Indian descent.
1962	Attended architectural training at the University of Guadalajara.
1966	Exhibition in Mexico City's Gallery Misrachi " Plastic Art."
1972	Lived and exhibited his art in Amsterdam.
1975	Formed artist group "Familia Studio Talier."
1977	Exhibited art, sculpture and clothing in United States and Europe.
1978	He began sculptures in brass and wood. He exhibited works in Houston, Sacramento, Hartford, and Seattle.
1979	He created his first furniture and silver sculptures.
1980	Exhibited his work in Montreal under the title of, "A Man And His Work."
1981	Introduced ceramics and bronze in his new works.
1982	Bustamante established "The Artes en Artesanias, S.A.," in Mexico.
1985	Featured in American Express advertisement "Do you know me?"
1986	Exhibited at the Museo National De La Mascara in San Louis Potosi. THE MEXICO OF SERGIO BUSTAMANTE, (Universal Press, Providence, RI).
1987	Designed the central sculpture of the Guadalajara Zoo.
1988	Permanent installation for Guadalajara Zoo.
1989	Opened galleries in Canada, Japan, United States, and Europe. EL MUNDO DE SERGIO BUSTAMANTE, (Galeria de Sergio Bustamante, Tokyo).
1994	Introduced jewelry designs.
1998	Studio and residence, Tlaquepaque, Mexico.

 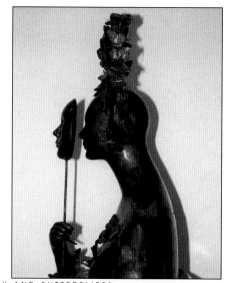

ABOVE: BRONZE "MASK AND BUTTERFLIES"
PREVIOUS TWO PAGES: "COACHALA (VERSION 2) WITH "MARCO ANGEL MIRROR"

C O A C H A L A

"The Coachala is originally from Tuxpan, Jalisco. At the beginning it was made with hen and corn dough by the natives of this region, the Nahuatl. Later it became well-known due to its easy cooking, economical and delightful; therefore; it was adopted by the population of this southern town of Ciudad Guzman, Jalisco, Mexico."

Version 1
serves 4-6

1 whole chicken, cooked and shredded (save the broth)

2 pounds lean pork meat, cooked and shredded

2 fresh long red chiles (such as chile chilacate)

5 dried long red chiles, soaked (such as chile chilacate)

1 cup rice, soaked in the chicken broth

1/2 pound corn dough or masa

1 medium bunch fresh cilantro (coriander leaves)

3 cloves garlic

2 pounds tomatoes, preferably violet variety

dry red hot chile to desired spiciness

cooking oil

salt to taste

chopped fresh cilantro for garnish

Liquefy tomatoes, garlic, cilantro, chiles, rice, and masa with chicken broth. Cook in oil stirring constantly and bring to a boil until thick in consistency. Season to taste. Add meat and remove from heat. Add cilantro and serve hot with freshly made tortillas.

Version 2
serves 2

1 chicken breast cooked in water and salt, shredded (save the broth)

1 pound lean pork meat, cooked in water and salt, shredded

3 or 4 ancho chiles

3 cloves garlic

1/4 medium onion

2 or 3 red tomatoes

15 to 20 violet tomatoes

1 tablespoon flour

1/4 pound corn dough or masa

Liquefy half of the shredded chicken breast with the previously sauteed chiles. If desired add 2-3 dry hot chiles for a spicier result. Saute onion until translucent and liquefy with red tomatoes, violet tomatoes and garlic. In a separate pan, cook flour in hot oil until golden in color, then add onion-tomato mixture. In a separate pan, stir together corn masa with chicken broth, strain and add to boiling tomato sauce. Salt to taste.

Add remaining chicken-chile mixture as well as the pork. For thinner consistency, add chicken broth.

Serve hot with fresh made tortillas.

Gold Margarita or Lime Daiquiri

SILVER NECKLACE

GOLD & SILVER CRUCIFIX

CALDER
PAINTER HILL ROAD
R. F. D. ROXBURY,
CONN.. U.S.A
TEL. & TEL. WOODBURY 1-2-3

1 NOV. 51

Dear Ed

I dont quite understand what you say about price — but will make you a mobile 4' across for $300.— . I really cant do it for any less, for we sell the very small ones for half that.

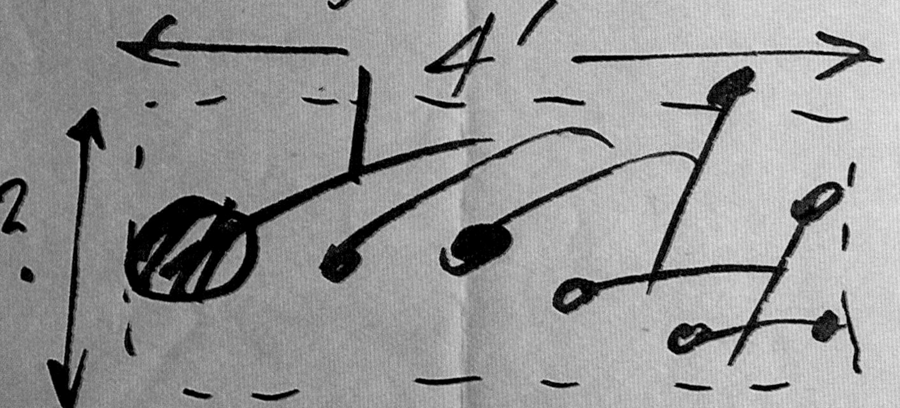

You say nothing about what color you might like. And

How about depth?

Cordially yours

Sandy

©1998 Artists Rights Society (ARS), New York/ADAGP, Paris

ABOVE: COURTSEY EDWARD DURELL STONE PAPERS, SPECIAL COLLECTIONS DIVISION, UNIVERSITY OF ARKANSAS LIBRARIES FAYETTEVILLE, AR CONCERNING PURCHASE OF MOBILES FOR THE FINE ARTS COMPLEX AT THE UNIVERISTY OF ARKANSAS SIX WERE PURCHASED AT A TOTAL COST OF $1300.
OPPOSITE: ORIGINAL MOBILE WITH DUCK CASSOULET AND APPLE TART   TOP: "FOUR ARCHES" SECURITY PACIFIC NATIONAL BANK, LOS ANGELES, 1974

©2008 Artists Rights Society (ARS), New York

"All my greatest admirers are under six."

1898   b. in Lawton, PA, of artist parents (mother- painter; father - sculptor).

1915   Graduated from the Stevens Institute of Technology in Hoboken, NJ with a degree in mechanical engineering.

1923   Entered Art Students League in NY and studied with Thomas Hart Benton, Guy Pène du Bois and John Sloan.

1925   Sold sketches of Barnum and Bailey Circus to "National Police Gazette."

1927   Lived in England and France continuing studies of the circus and animals.

1932   Introduced hand-cranked moving sculptures in Paris, he calls "MOBILES."

1943   Major exhibition for the "Museum of Modern Art" including new "painted wood and wire" scuptures called "CONSTELLATIONS."

1950   Designed sets for play "Happy as Larry."

1960   Recieved Gold Medal of the Architectural League of Arts and Letters, NY.

1968   Calder's ballet, "Work in Progress" opened in Rome.

1973   Painted planes "Flying Colors" Braniff International Airlines, Dallas, TX.

1975   Received United Nations Peace Medal, NYC.

1976   CALDER'S UNIVERSE, by Jean Lipman, (Viking Press, NYC).

1976   d. New York City, NY.

©1998 Artists Rights Society (ARS), New York/ADAGP, Paris

DUCK CASSOULET
Serves 4

4 each confit duck legs
(can be purchased at specialty
stores or markets)

4 cups cooked white beans

1 cup fresh pearl onions, peeled

1 pound smoked peppered
bacon, small dice

4 small links fresh andouille
sausage, or your favorite sausage

1 cup sun-dried tomatoes

1 ounce fresh thyme, picked from
stem and chopped fine

1 ounce fresh chives, chopped fine

2 heads roasted garlic, skin on,
cut in half

4 cups roasted chicken stock,
reduced by half

salt and pepper to taste

In a heavy-bottomed, non-reactive skillet, cook the bacon and sausage over medium-high heat, stirring until golden brown and cooked through.

Remove the sausage and bacon and reserve on a paper towel.

Discard all but two tablespoons of the fat and add the peeled pearl onions and cook over medium-high heat, turning to caramelize all sides.

Once the onions are caramelized, arrange the white beans, sausage and bacon, confit duck legs, sun-dried tomatoes, fresh chopped herbs, roasted heads of garlic and chicken stock in the same pan.

Bring the ingredients up to a simmer, season with salt and pepper to taste, and place in a pre-heated 350ºF oven.

Cook the cassoulet until chicken stock has reduced to a thick sauce consistency, approximately one hour.

Louis Latour Aloxe Corton 1993,
Cote-D'or, France

APPLE TART
Serves 4

1-10 inch x 15 inch puff pastry
sheet (can be found in the frozen
food section of your market)

4 Granny Smith apples, left whole,
cored and peeled

3 tablespoons melted butter

1 cup light brown sugar

1 cup white granulated sugar

Using a 10-inch plate as a stencil, cut a circle out of the puff pastry, and place on a non-stick baking sheet. Slice the apples horizontally 1/8-inch thick. Leaving a one inch border, shingle the apple slices evenly in a circular pattern until all slices are used covering the surface of the puff pastry. Brush the apples and the exposed pastry edge with melted butter. Mix the brown and white sugar, sprinkle evenly over the tart. Place in a pre-heated 350ºF oven and bake 15 to 20 minutes.

Bonny Doon, Muscat Canelli "Vin de Glacière,"
Santa Cruz, California

© CHRISTO/JEANNE CLAUDE © PHOTO WOLFGANG VOLTZ 1995

THIS PAGE: © 1995 CHRISTO/JEANNE-CLAUDE
"WRAPPED REICHSTAG, BERLIN, 1971-1995," PHOTOS
© WOLFGANG VOLTZ, OPPOSITE: "SURROUNDED
ISLANDS, BISCAYNE BAY, GREATER MIAMI," © 1983
CHRISTO/JEANNE-CLAUDE. PHOTO © WOLFGANG
VOLTZ WITH "TARATOR" IN ALVAR AALTO CRYSTAL
VASE, 1939

© CHRISTO/ JEANNE CLAUDE © PHOTO WOLFGANG VOLTZ

© CHRISTO/JEANNE-CLAUDE

"All our work is about freedom."

1935	Christo Javacheff: b. in Gabrovo, Bulgaria of industrialist parents.
1935	Jeanne-Claude: b. in Casablanca, Morocco, of a French military family.
1952	Jeanne-Claude: Baccalaureat in Latin and philosophy, University of Tunis.
1953	Christo studied at Fine Arts Academy, Sofia.
1957	Studied at Vienna Fine Arts Academy.
1962	"Iron Curtain-Wall of Oil Barrels" blocking the Rue Visconti, Paris. "Wrapping a Girl" London.
1964	Established permanent residence New York City.
1968	"Wrapped Fountain" and "Wrapped Medieval Tower" Spoleto.
1969	"Wrapped Museum of Contemporary Art" Chicago, IL.
1970	"Wrapped Monuments" Milano: "Monument to Vittorio Emanuele, Piazza Duomo; Monument to Leonardo daVinci, Piazza Scala."
1972	"Valley Curtain" Rifle, CO.
1976	"Running Fence" Sonoma and Marian Counties, CA.
1983	"Surrounded Islands" Biscayne Bay, Greater Miami, FL.
1985	"The Pont Neuf Wrapped" Paris.
1991	"The Umbrellas" Japan and United States.
1995	WRAPPED REICHSTAG, BERLIN by Christo / Jeanne-Claude, (Taschen Press, Cologne).
1998	Lives in New York City.

CHRISTO/JEANNE-CLAUDE "WRAPPED REICHSTAG," BERLIN 1971-1995
PHOTO © WOLFGANG VOLZ

T A R A T O R
(S U M M E R   S O U P)
serves 6

4-8 ounce containers plain
lowfat yogurt

1 cup walnuts, each walnut
cut into 8 pieces

1/2 cup fresh dill

2 tablespoons olive oil

2 tablespoons vinegar

4 large cucumbers, raw,
peeled and diced
as small as possible

1 teaspoon salt

Mix all ingredients together and refrigerate for at least 3 hours before serving.

Georges Duboeuf, Viognier Vin de Pays de
L'Ardéche 1994, Rhône, France.

ABOVE: "LA VENUS SPATIALE" BELOW: "ELEPHANT SPATIAL" EXHIBITION
IN THE PLACÉ VENDOME, PARIS. OPPOSITE: CRAYFISH CONSOMME AND BREAD

"Only by means of irrationality is it possible to re-endow things with their real value."

1904	b. Figueres, Spain, to a notary and wife.
1921	Attended the San Fernando Academy of Fine Arts in Madrid. Experimented with cubism.
1924	Imprisoned for 35 days in Girona for subversion.
1926	Traveled to Paris and met Picasso and Mirò, who introduced him to Dadaists and the Surrealist group.
1929	Met Gala Eluard, she became his lover, and muse.
1932	Exhibited "The Persistence of Memory" at Julien Levy Gallery, NY.
1934	Married Gala and opened one man show in London.
1936	Spanish Civil War forced him to leave Spain. Dali appeared on cover of TIME.
1943	Created first series of jewels for the Duke de Verdura.
1946	Worked with Walt Disney on a film "Destino" and designed dream sequences for Alfred Hitchcock's movie "Spellbound."
1952	Traveled throughout U.S. lecturing on nuclear mysticism.
1965	Illustrated for a new edition of the Bible.
1978	"Dali Lifting the Skin of the Mediterrean Sea to to Show Gala the Birth of Venus" exhibited at Guggenheim Museum, NYC.
1982	Salvador Dali Museum opened in St. Petersburg, FL.
1989	d. in Figueres, Spain.

"LE PROFIL DU TEMPO" IN PLACÉ VENDOME, PARIS

△

CRAYFISH CONSOMMÉ
Serves 6-8

3 pounds crayfish (or shrimp)

3 cups dry red wine

3 quarts water

1/2 cup dry sherry

1 tablespoon cayenne pepper

2 tablespoons paprika

pinch saffron

1 pound veal or pork, chopped

2 cups rice

4 egg whites

1 teaspoon salt

In a large pot add the red wine, water, salt, cayenne pepper, saffron, meat and rice. While bringing to a boil, blend the crayfish in a food processor with a little water. Then add the crayfish or shrimp slowly to the large pot and simmer it for 45 minutes. Pour mixture through a sieve, reserving the liquid - in a medium sauce pan. Reheat sauce pan and stir while slowly adding the egg whites (do not let boil.) Let the cooked eggs settle and gently pour off the cleared crayfish consommè. Serve with garlic bread.

Veuve Clicquot Yellow Label N/V, Reims, France

△

GARLIC BREAD
Serves 4

1 large loaf French bread

2 tablespoons fresh
chopped garlic

1/4 cup extra virgin olive oil

salt and pepper to taste

Split the bread lengthwise. Mix the olive oil and garlic. Spread evenly on the two sides of the bread. Season with salt and pepper to taste. Place on a non-stick baking sheet in a pre-heated 350ºF oven and cook until golden brown.

"We have incorporated the foods of the earth from the Plains Indians, the foods of the soul from the Northern Mexicans, and the foods of substance from the American Cowboys into our very own Southwest Cuisine."

1945	b. Louisville, Kentucky of inn keeper parents.
1965	Classically trained at the Culinary Institute of America, Hyde Park, NY.
1967	Maisonette in Cincinnati followed by the Pyramid Room, Fairmont Hotel, Dallas, TX.
1980	Executive Sous chef at the Mansion on Turtle Creek, Dallas, TX.
1982	Chef and part owner of Agnew's restaurant.
1985	Returned to The Mansion to become executive chef.
1987	Published THE MANSION ON TURTLE CREEK CUSINE, (Grove Press, NY).
1990	DEAN FEARING'S SOUTHWEST CUISINE, (Grove Weidenfeld Press, Inc., NYC).
1994	Robb Report "Best U.S. Restaurant." (The Mansion on Turtle Creek)
1998	Lives in Dallas, Texas.

• •

BEEF TENDERLOIN MARINATED IN MOLASSES AND BLACK PEPPER, SERVED WITH COMPOTE OF SMOKED BACON, WILD MUSHROOMS, GLAZED SWEET POTATOES, AND PECANS

Serves 4

2 pounds center-cut beef tenderloin (or venison), trimmed of all fat and silver skin

1 cup molasses

2 tablespoons balsamic vinegar

2 tablespoons fresh cracked black pepper

2 cloves garlic, peeled and finely chopped

1 large shallot, peeled and finely chopped

2 teaspoons fresh ginger, finely grated

1 teaspoon fresh thyme, finely chopped

crushed red pepper flakes to taste

salt to taste

2 tablespoons vegetable oil

Compote of Smoked Bacon, Wild Mushrooms, Glazed Sweet Potatoes, and Pecans (recipe follows)

4 sprigs fresh watercress

Place beef tenderloin in a glass dish. In a small bowl, combine molasses, balsamic vinegar, black pepper, garlic, shallot, ginger, thyme, and pepper flakes. When well blended, reserve 1/2 cup of marinade, pour over beef. Cover. Refrigerate, allowing meat to marinate, for 24 hours, turning occasionally.

Remove meat from marinade, reserving 1/2 cup for Smoked Bacon Compote and 4 tablespoons to deglaze pan. Place on cutting board, and using sharp knife, cut into 8 portions. Season with salt.

Heat oil in a large cast-iron skillet over medium-high heat. When hot, lay beef medallions in skillet and brown for 3 minutes.

Turn and brown for 2 minutes or until desired degree of doneness is reached. Just before removing meat, add 4 tablespoons reserved molasses marinade to skillet to deglaze the pan as well as to glaze the medallions. Quickly turn meat over to glaze other side. Remove from skillet immediately.

To Assemble:
Place 2 medallions near the center of each of four hot serving plates, overlapping each other. Spoon the smoked bacon compote next to the medallions, letting the sauce flow out onto the plate.

Place a sprig of watercress in between the meat and the compote. Serve immediately.

For Compote of Smoked Bacon, Wild Mushrooms, Glazed Sweet Potatoes, and Pecans:

1/2 cup reserved molasses marinade

1 cup veal demi-glace (or beef stock)

1 cup smoked slab bacon, cut into 1/2 in. dice

1 tablespoon vegetable oil

2 cups wild mushrooms (any type)

2 tablespoons unsalted butter

1 cup sweet potato balls

1/2 to 3/4 cup pearl onions, peeled

1 tablespoon brown sugar

2 tablespoons cider vinegar

1/2 cup Glazed Pecans (recipe follows)

salt to taste

PREVIOUS TWO PAGES: FIRST:"BANANA TACOS" SECOND: "BEEF TENDERLOIN WITH PECANS AND WILD MUSHROOMS" fresh lemon juice to taste

Reduce reserved marinade in a small saucepan over medium-high heat for 5 minutes or until reduced by half. Add demi-glace or beef stock and bring to a boil. Lower heat and simmer for 5 minutes or until sauce coats the back of a spoon. Remove from heat and keep warm. Render bacon in a small sauté pan over medium-high heat. When hot, add mushrooms and sauté for 3 minutes or until cooked.

Preheat oven to 350 F. Melt butter in an ovenproof medium sauté pan over medium heat. When hot, add sweet potato balls and pearl onions. Sauté for 3 minutes. Add brown sugar and cider vinegar and stir to combine. Sauté for 2 minutes.

Place pan in oven and cook for 7 minutes, stirring occasionally to glaze evenly.

Remove from oven. add bacon, mushrooms, reduced marinade, and Glazed Pecans. Stir to combine. Season with salt and lemon juice and serve.

For Glazed Pecans:

1/2 cup water

1/2 cup sugar

2 dried red chilies

1 cup whole fresh pecans

1/4 cup molasses

Preheat oven to 250ºF.

Combine water, sugar, and chilies in a small saucepan over high heat. Bring to a boil. Add pecans and return to a boil. Lower heat and simmer for 10 minutes.

Drain and place pecans on a baking sheet. Place in preheated oven and bake for 45 minutes, stirring occasionally. Remove pecans from oven and pour into a small bowl. Add molasses and toss to coat. Return nuts to baking sheet and place in oven. Bake for an additional 45 minutes or until pecans are very crisp and crunchy but not burned.

Louis M. Martini "Gnarly Vine" Zinfandel 1994, Sonoma Valley, California

BANANA SOFT TACOS WITH GRAND MARNIER GLAZE AND PAPAYA AND STRAWBERRY SALSAS
Serves 4

1 cup cake flour

1 cup bread flour

2 tablespoons sugar

pinch of salt

2 cups milk

4 large eggs, beaten

4 large egg yolks, beaten

1/2 cup unsalted butter, melted and still hot

1/4 cup cognac

Glazed Bananas (recipe follows)

Grand Marnier Glaze (recipe follows)

Papaya Salsa (recipe follows)

Strawberry Salsa (recipe follows)

In a mixing bowl, combine both flours, sugar, and salt. Slowly beat in milk, eggs, and egg yolks. Whisk in butter, then cognac. Stir well to combine. Allow to sit for 15 to 20 minutes. Lightly butter an 8 inches sauté or crêpe pan and place over medium heat. Pour in approximately 1 tablespoon batter and swirl in a circular motion to cover bottom of pan. Cook for 2 to 3 minutes or until lightly browned. Turn crêpe over and cook for an additional 2 to 3 minutes. Continue until all batter is used. Do not stack crêpes one on top of the other or they will stick together.

Preheat broiler. Prepare Glazed Bananas, Grand Marnier glaze and salses. Spoon 6 or 8 slices of Glazed Banana in the center of each crêpe and roll up like a soft taco. Place 2 on each of four ovenproof serving plates. Pour Grand Marnier Glaze across the top of the tacos and place under preheated broiler for 2 minutes or until lightly browned. Spoon 4 or 5 more banana slices on top and serve with Papaya and Strawberry Salsas on the side.

For Glazed Bananas:

1/2 cup unsalted butter

1 cup packed light brown sugar

2 tablespoons fresh orange juice

2 tablespoons Grand Marnier

6 bananas, peeled and sliced

Combine butter and brown sugar in a small saucepan over medium heat. Cook for 3 minutes or until liquefied. Stir in orange juice and Grand Marnier and cook for 5 minutes. Remove from heat and stir in sliced bananas. Serve warm.

For Grand Marnier Glaze:

5 large egg yolks

1/4 cup sugar

3 tablespoons Grand Marnier

Beat egg yolks and sugar in the top half of a double boiler over simmering water for 10 minutes or until ribbon consistency is reached. Remove from heat and cool slightly. Whisk in Grand Marnier.

For Papaya Salsa:

1 papaya, peeled, halved and seeded

3 tablespoons sugar

1 teaspoon ground cinnamon

Cut one papaya half into 1/4 inch dice and set aside. In a blender, purée remaining half with sugar and cinnamon. Pour purée over diced papaya and stir to combine. Set aside.

For Strawberry Salsa:

1 pint strawberries, washed and hulled

3 tablespoons light brown sugar

Cut one half of the strawberries into 1/4-inch dice. Set aside. In a blender, purée remaining strawberries with brown sugar. Pour purée over diced strawberries. Stir to combine. Set aside.

Recipes continue on page 226.

ABOVE: LOBBY OF "THE BANK OF HONG KONG" BELOW: HONG KONG CURRENCY WITH BANK OF HONG KONG ENGRAVED ELEVATION OPPOSITE: "SPAGHETTI AL PESTO" WITH "THE BANK OF HONG KONG" IN BACKGROUND

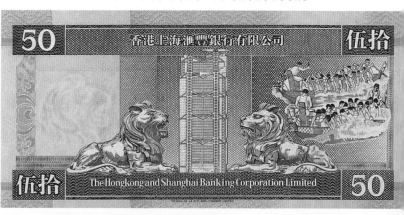

"What excites me are really the ingredients of architecture. It's a bit like being a chef, you don't need expensive materials or grand opportunities to have a feast. And that, I believe, is true of architecture."

1935	b. Manchester, England.
1956	University of Manchester, School of Architecture and Department of Town and Country Planning.
1960	Joined Royal Air Force.
1962	Post Graduate studies at Yale University School of Architecture, New Haven, CT.
1963	Worked as "Team 4" with wife Wendy, and Su and Richard Rogers.
1967	Formed architectural firm "Foster Associates."
1979	"Hong Kong Bank," Hong Kong.
1982	Worked with Buckminister Fuller on "Autonomous House."
1983	Exhibition "Three New Skyscrapers," The Museum of Modern Art, NY.
1988	"Telecommunications Tower," Torre di Collserola, Barcelona.
1991	"Stansted International Airport," Essex, England.
1992	FOSTER ASSOCIATES: RECENT WORKS (Academy Editions/St. Martin's Press, London).
1994	Awarded "Gold Medal," The American Institute of Architects.
1997	"Chek Lap Kok Airport," Hong Kong.
1998	Lives in London.

STANSTED INTERNATIONAL AIRPORT, ESSEX, ENGLAND

SPAGHETTI AL PESTO
serves 4

1/2 pound fresh basil leaves

1 tablespoon fresh chopped garlic

4 ounces toasted pine nuts

4 ounces fresh grated
parmesan cheese

1 teaspoon salt

1 teaspoon fresh ground
black pepper

Place all the ingredients in a food processor and purée, occasionaly scraping down the sides with a rubber spatula, until smooth. Remove and place in an air-tight container. Refrigerate until needed. This pesto will keep for up to two weeks under refrigeration and freezes well also. Toss pesto with 1 pound "Aldente" cooked spaghetti.

Chateau Potelle "VGS" Chardonnay 1994,
Mt. Veeder, California

STANSTED INTERNATIONAL AIRPORT, ESSEX, ENGLAND

ABOVE: "SHAMAN WITH BEAR SKULL" AT "INN AT THE MILL"   OPPOSITE: "MAD MAX'S GRILLED RAINBOW TROUT"/ "DUCKCATCHER"

"As our imagination is freed to receive greater truths, then fear, closed thinking, and poverty of spirit will be left behind."

1942	b. Morrilton, Arkansas.
1964	Received Bachelor of Fine Arts degree from University of Texas at Austin.
1966	Received Masters of Fine Arts degree from Universtiy of Dallas, Irving, TX.
1968	Received Masters of Fine Arts degree from University of Kansas, Lawrence, KS.
1969	Mid-America I Exhibition, Kansas City, MO (Sculpture Award)
1975	"The Duck Catcher" 4' bronze.
1976	"Shaman with Bear Skull" 7' bronze.
	Exhibition Museum of Fine Arts, Riverside, CA.
1980	"The West Returns to Grand Central" Grand Central Gallery, NY.
1981	Solo Exhibition, Smithsonian Institution, Washington, DC.
1982	Exhibition First Contemporary International Exhibition, Chico, CA.
1985	Western Artists Exhibition, Lubbock, TX, "Gold Medal."
1986	Texas Cowboy Artists "Gold Medal."
1987	National Cowboy Hall of Fame, Sculpture Exhibition.
1988	Solo Exhibition, Kennedy Galleries, NY.
1989	"Dream Flight" 15' bronze for the Albuquerque International Airport.
1990	"Fellow" of National Sculpture Society.
1991	"Strength of One" 14' bronze fountain, near Montgomery, AL.
1996	"Global Family Tree of Life" 32', Sanctioned by U.N.E.P., Nagoya, Japan.
1998	Lives with wife Rachelle in Paonia, Colorado.

MAQUETTE FOR "DREAM FLIGHT," 15' BRONZE IN
THE ALBUQUERQUE INTERNATIONAL AIRPORT

"This recipe comes from a serious gourmet cook - a friend from graduate school days who teaches at the School for American Crafts in Rochester, NY - whose gourmet skills make you think you would have to go to heaven to taste anything better."

– Rachelle Fox

"It would be impossible to exaggerate the incredible flavor of this dish - a simple marinade of basil, rosemary and olive oil give to this trout. . . This is so easy and positively wonderful anytime of the year! Serve with roasted red potatoes, a Belgian endive and red leaf salad dressed with a good olive oil and your favorite flavored vinegar, and warm sourdough bread."

– Lincoln Fox

MAD MAX'S GRILLED RAINBOW TROUT
Serves 4

4 select small rainbow trout

salt

fresh ground black pepper
(somewhat coarse)

1/4 cup extra virgin olive oil

2 tablespoons fresh squeezed
lemon juice

2 small sprigs fresh rosemary
or basil chopped very fine
or substitute approximately 1/2
teaspoon dried rosemary or basil

1/2 cup fine bread crumbs

Clean the trout in cold water, then pat dry with paper towels. Salt and pepper the trout on both sides and place them in a tray. Sprinkle olive oil, fresh lemon juice and the rosemary or basil over the trout.

"RAM SHAMAN"

The fish should be turned over at least three times to coat well.

Sprinkle the bread crumbs over the trout and turn, ensuring an even coating on both sides.

The bread crumbs should soak up the oil. Refrigerate in the marinade for at least 2 hours, turning occasionally. Prior to broiling, let the trout come to room temperature and reserve marinade for basting.

Preheat the grill for at least 15 minutes before you are ready to cook.

Use a fish grilling rack and grill flesh side down for about 3 minutes. Turn and cook another 3 to 4 minutes.

Baste with the reserved marinade. If the trout is thicker it will take longer to grill.

Serve with lemon wedges.

Caymus Conundrum 1996, California

for Courtney
michael graves
1994

ABOVE: DRAWING FOR COURTNEY "THE PLACE I'LL RETIRE TO" OPPOSITE: "CHAMPAGNE, ASPARAGUS, AND WILD MUSHROOM RISOTTO" AT WALT DISNEY WORLD SWAN/DOLPHIN RESORTS, WALT DISNEY WORLD, FL.

42

"I always begin a project by thinking about use and symbol simultaneously."

1934	b. Indianapolis, Indiana. Father a livestock broker, mother a nurse.
1958	Graduated from University of Cincinnati, Department of Architecture.
1959	Master's Degree in Architecture from Harvard.
1960	Won Rome Prize (Prix di Roma), The American Academy in Rome.
1962	Began teaching at Princeton University.
1964	Joined Richard Meier, Peter Eisenman, John Hejduk and Charles Gwathmey as the "New York Five."
1969	Exhibited at the Museum of Modern Art, NYC.
1975	"Plocek Residence" in Warren Township, New Jersey, established him as the founder of the Post Modernism movement in architecture.
1979	Designed furniture and showrooms for Sunar.
1980	"Resident Architect," The American Academy in Rome.
1982	MICHAEL GRAVES: BUILDINGS AND PROJECTS. 1966-1981, (Rizzoli, Int, NYC).
1983	Designed "Portland Building" in Portland, OR and "Humana Building" in Louisville, KY.
1984	"Clos Pegase Winery," Calistoga, CA.
1986	Designed the "Dolphin" and "Swan" Hotels for Walt Disney World in Orlando, FL. Also "Hotel New York," Euro-Disney, France.
1990	MICHAEL GRAVES: BUILDINGS AND PROJECTS 1982-1989, (Princeton Architectural Press, Princeton, NJ)
1994	Opened first store featuring his product arts, in Princeton, NJ. MICHAEL GRAVES (Ernst and Sohn / St. Martins Press, NYC)
1998	Lives in Princeton, New Jersey.

MILES AND COURTNEY AT CLOS PEGASE WINERY, CALISTOGA, CA

△
CHAMPAGNE RISOTTO
serves 6

4 cups chicken broth

4 cups "brut" champagne

6 tablespoons butter

1 medium onion, chopped finely

2 1/2 cups arborio rice

1 cup grated parmesan cheese

salt and pepper to taste

garnish with caviar

Heat chicken broth in a medium sauce pan. Sauté onions in a large sauce pan with 3 tablespoons butter until pale yellow. Add rice and coat with butter, add 2 cups champagne. Sauté until wine has evaporated. Stir in enough broth to cover rice. Stir over medium heat until moisture is absorbed. Continue cooking and stirring rice, adding broth a little at a time as it is absorbed, about 10 minutes. For the next ten minutes cook the mixutre, adding slowly the remaining champagne, only adding liquid as it is absorbed. Rice is done when tender and firm to the bite. While hot, stir in 1/2 cup parmesan cheese and 3 tablespoons butter. Salt and pepper to taste. Place in a warm dish and serve immediately with the remaining parmesan cheese. If desired garnish with a teaspoon of caviar with each serving.

> Clos Pegase, Chardonnay 1994,
> Napa Valley, California

△
WILD MUSHROOM RISOTTO
serves 6

7 cups chicken broth

1/2 pound fresh mushrooms, thinly sliced (such as oyster, shiitake, portabello, morel, chanterelle) stems removed, reserved for later

1 cup dried wild mushrooms (such as porcini, morel or black trumpet), ground in a spice mill or coffee grinder

7 tablespoons butter

1 medium onion, chopped finely

2 1/2 cups arborio rice

3/4 cup dry red wine

1/2 cup grated parmesan cheese

2 teaspoons fresh chopped thyme

salt and pepper to taste

Sauté fresh mushrooms in 2 tablespoons butter until golden, set aside. Heat chicken broth in a meduim sauce pan with 3 tablespoons butter until caramelized. Add rice and coat with butter, add wine. Sauté until wine is evaporated. Stir in enough broth to cover rice. Stir over medium heat until moisture is absorbed. Continue cooking and stirring, adding broth a little at a time unti it is absorbed, about 20 minutes. Rice is done when tender and firm to the bite. Stir in mushrooms, parmesan cheese, and remaining butter. Place in a warm dish, serve immediately. Top with parmesan cheese.

△
ASPARAGUS RISOTTO
serves 6

5 cups chicken broth

1 pound pencil sized asparagus

1 stick plus 3 tablespoons butter

1/2 pound fresh spinach leaves

1 medium onion, chopped finely

2 1/2 cups arborio rice

1/2 cup dry white wine

1/2 cup grated parmesan cheese

1/4 cup water

1 tablespoon olive oil

salt and pepper to taste

Clean asparagus and cut in half. Roughly chop the bottoms, sauté in olive oil with half of the onion. When onion becomes translucent, add spinach, one stick of butter, season with salt and pepper, add water. Bring to a simmer. Transfer to a blender, purée, pass through a seive. Reserve warm. Heat chicken broth. Sauté onions in a large pan with 3 tablespoons butter until translucent. Add rice, coat with butter, add wine. Sauté until wine is evaporated. Stir in enough broth to cover rice. Stir over medium heat until moisture is absorbed. Continue stirring, adding broth a little at a time until rice is tender but firm to the bite, about 10 minutes. While hot, stir in asparagus tips, asparagus butter and 1/2 cup parmesan cheese. Add salt and pepper.

DENVER CITY LIBRARY, DENVER, CO

ABOVE: "SEQUI" 1986, 10 x12.5 x 5 FEET, BRONZE W/POLYCHROME PATINA, AT THE WELLS FARGO CENTER, LOS ANGELES, CA OPPOSITE: "CARROT SOUP AND TOSTADAS"

©NANCY GRAVES FOUNDATION/LICENSED BY VAGA, NEW YORK, NY.

"I think in any good work there is humor."

1940	b. Pittsfield, Massachusetts.
1961	Bachelor of Arts, Vassar College, Poughkeepsie, NY.
1964	Bachelor of Fine Arts and Master of Arts, Yale University.
1965	Fulbright-Hayes Grant in Painting, Paris.
1969	Exhibition, Whitney Museum of Art, NY.
1971	Vassar College Fellowship Paris Biennale Grant.
1971	Exhibition, the Museum of Modern Art, NY.
1973	Exhibition, The National Gallery of Canada, Ottawa.
1975	Exhibition, Janie C. Lee Gallery, Houston, TX.
1978	"Resident in Painting," American Academy in Rome.
1980	Skowhegan Medal for Drawing Graphics.
1981	Exhibition, Knoedler Gallery, New York City, NY.
	1981-1983, 1985, 1986, 1988-1997
1988	Exhibition, Gallery Mukai, Tokyo, Japan.
1992	Honorary Doctor of Fine Arts Degree, Yale University.
	NANCY GRAVES: EXCAVATIONS IN PRINT by Thomas Padon, (Abrams, NYC, 1996).
1995	d. New York.

"BRIDGED (SPILL SERIES)" 1983, 24.5 x 30.5 x 12 INCHES, BRONZE W/POLYCHROME PATINA

©NANCY GRAVES FOUNDATION/LICENSED BY VAGA, NEW YORK, NY

CARROT SOUP
Serves 4

1 pound fresh carrots

1 tablespoon unsalted butter

2 tablespoons chopped onion

4 cups stock
(vegetable or chicken) or water

3 tablespoons rice
(or the equivalent of stale white
bread, crusts removed)

Cut the carrots into thin slices and gently cook them (in half the butter) together with the onions. When they are tender, add the liquid and the rice or bread. Simmer for 20 minutes, then pass them through a sieve, adding more liquid if the puree is too stiff. Reheat, add the remaining butter and serve with golden croutons.

(Salt to taste.)

RICE SALAD

1/2 cup chestnuts, baked or
steamed, then peeled
and chopped

1 cup cooked brown rice, cooled

1 head romaine lettuce, torn

1/2 bunch fresh spinach, torn

1 cup grated carrot

1 red bell pepper, chopped fine

1 small bunch green onions,
chopped fine (tops only)

1/8 cup parsley, chopped fine

1/2 cup green peas

1 cup alfalfa sprouts

Prepare chestnuts and cool. Prepare rice and cool. Mix vegetables and rice together in a large bowl.

Add avocado dressing (see below) and mix together. Sprinkle chestnut pieces over top and serve.

AVOCADO SALAD DRESSING

Mash 2 ripe avocados into a smooth paste with a small amount of water or lemon juice. Use as a spread over the rice salad. (Salt to taste).

TOSTADAS

2 ripe avocados, mashed

1 bunch fresh spinach

1/4 cup fresh chives

1 bunch broccoli,
tops only chopped coarsely

1/2 cup green peas

6-8 corn tortillas

2 cups alfalfa sprouts

Lightly steam the vegetables. Place corn tortillas in oven at 450° F until crispy. Add mashed avocado on each tortilla.

Ferrari-Carano Fumé Blanc 1996,
Sonoma County, California

Add steamed vegetables on top, then add grated carrot and sprouts on top. Season if desired and serve.

LENTIL ARTICHOKE SURPRISE

2 cups lentil sprouts

1 head broccoli, cut in pieces

4 artichokes

2 stalks celery, chopped fine

1 head romaine lettuce

Steam artichokes. Remove leaves and chokes and cut hearts into pieces. Steam lentil sprouts and broccoli.

Mix all the above together. Add finely chopped celery. Serve on lettuce leaves or wrap lettuce around mixture to make "sandwich."

FROZEN BANANA CREME

This recipe requires a Champion juicer (1 ripe banana per serving). Buy and peel fully ripened bananas. Freeze bananas hard in a plastic bag or container.

Install the solid plastic panel beneath the juicer barrel, and place a bowl beneath the juicer spout.

Feed frozen bananas into juicer. Serve and enjoy the amazing taste and consistancy of this treat and its similarity to ice cream.

"ISO DANCE COMPANY, 1990, DANIEL EZRALOW, ASHLEY ROLAND, JAMEY HAMPTON, SHEILA LEHNER" WITH "PECAN CRUSTED SWORDFISH" ON "PHILIPPE STARCK'S STAINLESS STEEL TRAY" FOR ALESSI. OPPOSITE: PHOTO ©1990 LOIS GREENFIELD, BILL T. JONES & ARNIE, ZANE DANCE CO. 1983/SWEDISH PANCAKES WITH BERRIES

PHOTO © 1983 LOIS GREENFIELD

"It intrigues me that in 1/500th of a second I can allude to past and future moments even if these are only imagined."

1949	b. New York City.
1966	Studied anthropology and film making at Brandeis University, Waltham MA.
1970	Started working as a photo journalist in Boston.
1973	Began to photograph dance for the Village voice, New York Times and other magazines.
1980	Opened studio in NYC to photograph dance in the studio, rather than in the theater.
1982	Photographed young dancers David Parsons and Daniel Ezralow using a square format Hasselblad camera.
1992	BREAKING BOUNDS, THE DANCE PHOTOGRAPHY OF LOIS GREENFIELD, (published by Thames and Hudson, UK and Chronicle Books, USA). One Woman Show at the International Center of Photography, NYC.
1998	Her work is currently exhibited througout the world in galleries and museums. AIRBORNE, A NEW MONOGRAPH, By Lois Greenfield, (published by Thames Hudson UK and Chronicle Books, USA). She lives in New York City with her husband and two teenage sons.

SELF-PORTRAIT WITH DANIEL EZRALOW AND DAVID PARSONS, PHOTO © LOIS GREENFIELD, 1983

◇
PECAN CASHEW GLAZED SWORDFISH
Serves 4

4 swordfish filets

1 cup roasted cashews, unsalted

1 cup pecans

2/3 cup light brown sugar

Juice of half a lime

Freshly ground pepper to taste

1/3 cup olive oil

1 small red onion, chopped fine

1/2 cup honey

4 sprigs fresh thyme

Juice of 1 lime

1 1/4 cups Rose's lime juice

Preheat oven to 450ºF. In a food processor, combine nuts and process until coarsely chopped. Place in a mixing bowl and add the brown sugar, juice of half a lime, pepper and olive oil. Mix the nut glaze with your hands until it forms a tight ball.

Cover each steak with the glaze, pressing down to create an even topping. Set aside while preparing the sauce. In a saucepan, combine the onion, honey, thyme and juice from the whole lime, bringing the mixture to a boil.

Reduce the heat and cook until the sauce is red, glossy and will cling to a spoon. Remove from heat and keep warm. Roast steaks at 450ºF, preferably on a wet cedar wood plank, until the nuts have browned, approximately 7 to 10 minutes. Top

each steak with a small amount of the caramelized onion sauce. Serve with lemon beurre blanc.

– Courtesy of Michael Caracciolo and Dereck Brewley of India House Restaurant, Nantucket, MA

Chateau de Puligny-Montrachet Meursault
Les Perrières 1995, Côte de Beaune, France

△
SWEDISH PANCAKES
Makes 12 to 15 pancakes

2 eggs

1/2 cup milk

1 tablespoon clarified butter, melted, (unsalted), more is needed for cooking pancakes

1/2 cup all-purpose flour

1/4 teaspoon salt

Optional:
1 tablespoon sugar if making dessert pancakes

In a food processor, mix all ingredients at high speed for 1 minute, scraping down sides once or twice. Refrigerate 45 minutes.

For 5-inch pancakes, put 1/4 cup batter onto a hot, buttered skillet or pan. Cook over medium heat until surface is bubbly. Turn pancake over and cook until golden, about 30 seconds. Remove and stack until ready to use. (They may be frozen and thawed in a microwave when needed.)

Serve warm with butter and sweetened lingonberries or raspberries. Or fold into quarters and serve with a dusting of powdered sugar.

MURAL © RICHARD HAAS / LICENSED BY VAGA/NEW YORK, NY

"FOUNTAINBLEAU," 1986, MIAMI BEACH. OPPOSITE: "FISH PIROGUE AND BORSCHT" AT "CASCADES," 1985 (DEMOLISHED SUMMER 1996)

RICHARD HAAS PUBLISHED BY VAGA/NEW YORK

RICHARD HAAS

ARTIST

"In a way I am like a doctor or surgeon binding up the wounds of the city."

1936	b. Spring Green, Wisconsin.
1959	Bachelor of Science, University of Wisconsin, Milwaukee, WI.
1964	Masters of Fine Arts, University of Minnesota.
1974	Exhibition, Whitney Museum of American Art, NY.
1977	The American Institute of Architects, Medal of Honor.
1980	Exhibition, "Richard Haas; Architectural Facades" San Francisco Museum of Modern Art, CA.
1983	Received Guggenheim Fellowship.
1985	Exhibition, "Architecture of Illusion" The Aspen Art Museum, Aspen, CO.
1986	Facade painting, "Fountainbleau" Hilton Hotel, Miami Beach, FL.
1989	"Richard Haas; Architectural Projects 1974-1988" Brook Alexander Gallery, NYC.
1991	Honorary PH.D., University of Wisconsin, Milwaukee, WI.
1996	Architectural Paintings for state of Florida, Tallahassee and Jacksonville, FL.
1998	Lives with his wife Katherine Sokolnikoff in New York City.

"CASCADES," 1985 MURALS BY RICHARD HAAS, (BAKERY CENTER) MIAMI, FL., (DEMOLISHED SUMMER OF 1996)

MURAL © RICHARD HAAS/ LICENSED BY VAGA/NEW YORK, NY

FISH PIROGUE

"This is a Russian recipe for a Fish Pirogue (boat in Russian). Pirogues can be made with meat, fish or fruit. This is a small recipe, serving approximately three hungry people. I usually double this for eight and serve an appetizer or soup, salad and dessert and no one is hungry."

–Katherine Sokolnikoff Haas

For the Dough:

one dry yeast cake

1 cup milk, lukewarm

2 tablespoons sugar, heaping

1 teaspoon salt

2 tablespoons butter, melted
(or use unflavored cooking oil)

2 eggs, lightly beaten

4 cups bread flour

For the Filling:

1 medium onion, thinly sliced

2 tablespoons butter

1 cup cooked rice
(approximately 1/3 cup raw rice)

2 hard boiled eggs, chopped

2 tablespoons pearl tapioca

1 small bunch parsley, chopped
("enough chopped parsley to
make finished mixture
attractively green")

1 pound fresh, sweet smelling,
mixed white fish fillets
(such as halibut, sole, flounder,
sand dabs or bass)

2 tablespoons butter

Salt and pepper to taste

For Assembly:

about 1/2 cup fine bread
or cracker crumb

1 egg, beaten
with 1 tablespoon water

butter

First prepare the dough, by crumbling the yeast cake into 1 cup lukewarm milk. Stir until smooth. Add the sugar, salt, melted butter or oil, and beaten eggs. Stir in the bread flour. Set this aside in a warm place, covered, to rise. When approximately doubled in bulk, turn onto a floured board and with oiled hands knead the dough until smooth and elastic. Turn it back into a greased bowl and cover with a cloth, let it rise again in the warm place until doubled in volume. Next prepare the filling by sautéing the onion in butter until transparent. Set aside. Add boiling water to the tapioca, stirring and mashing, until it is of a workable consistency.

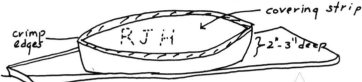

Add water as needed so it does not clump. In a medium mixing bowl, gently mix cooled cooked rice, cooked onion, tapioca, eggs and parsley. Salt and pepper to taste. Set aside. Sauté the fish fillets in butter until almost done. Salt and pepper to taste.

The Making of the Pirogue:
This quantity will fill an 8 x 8 inch pan. Double it, and you can make this rather elastic dough fit a 9 x 13 inch pan. (After a run using a pan, the brave might try to work without a pan directly on a baking sheet. To do so lay the dough out on a greased baking sheet, trim off a covering strip, add the filling ingredients and then seal the pirogue up, pinching the edges together. When doing this, shape the dough into a row boat-like form, with a point at bow and stern and use the final covering strip to make the top. Preheat oven to 350 F. When ready to assemble the Pirogue, turn the dough out onto a floured board and roll out approximately 1/4 inch thick. Grease the baking pan with butter and sprinkle with cracker crumbs. Place the dough in the pan, ensuring there is sufficient overhang to eventually cover all ingredients. Add a layer of the rice mixture (about half), dot with butter, add salt and pepper to taste. Gently place slightly cooked fish in an even layer filling the pan edge to edge. Top with remaining rice mixture, more dots of butter, salt and pepper. Now with completely dry, clean hands stretch the dough to entirely cover the filling, pinch all edges together. If there is excess

dough, trim it off. Brush the top of the assembled pirogue with the beaten egg. As this dish is usually for a special birthday meal; cut the initials of the birthday person into the top in as grand and decorative way as possible. Place in oven and bake for about 35 minutes or until nicely browned on top.

Do not over cook or you will destroy the fish. Place on a rack until cool enough to handle, then invert very carefully onto a board, and turn onto another board or serving platter so decorative top is facing up. Let pirogue rest covered with a clean towel for about half an hour so filling will firm up before serving.

BORSCHT
serves 2-4

4 large beets, chopped finely

2 onions, chopped finely

1 quart water

juice of 1 large lemon

1/2 cup sour cream

dash of sugar

Add chopped beets and chopped onions into water, bring to a boil. Reduce to simmer, cook for 40 minutes, (or until beets are tender). Blend in a food processor until smooth while adding lemon juice, sugar and salt to taste. Serve hot or cold, topped with sour cream.

FROZEN VODKA
WITH ROSES
serves 4

Boil 2 quarts of water and let cool (this makes the ice clear). Open the top of an empty 1/2 gallon milk or juice container, wash the container. In the upright container place a bottle of good quality vodka. Carefully arrange flowers around the bottle, keeping them below the rim of the container. Gently pour water over the flowers to within 1/2 inch of the top. Freeze overnight. Run warm water over frozen container to remove ice block. Return to freezer until ready to use.

©1991 THE ESTATE OF KEITH HARING

"My father was my main inspiration to be an artist and then Disney, Warhol, and Picasso."

1958	b. Kutztown, Pennsylvania. His father drew him cartoons.
1976	Studied briefly at a commercial art school.
	Exhibited his abstract paintings at the Pittsburgh Center for the Arts.
1978	Moved to New York City and studied at the School of Visual Arts.
1981	Began chalk drawings in New York subway stations.
	Met graffiti artist LA II (Angel Oritz).
1982	Drew a 30 second animation for Spectacolor Billboard, Times Square, NYC.
1983	Exhibited in Whitney Museum, NYC. Met Andy Warhol.
	Painted Fiorucci store, Milan, with LA II.
1984	Painted murals in Australia, Brazil and United States.
1985	Exhibited painted steel sculptures at Leo Castelli Gallery, NYC.
1986	Created "Andy Mouse" series combining his admiration for both Disney and Warhol. Opened Pop Shop in NYC. Paints on "Berlin Wall."
1987	Artist-in-residence and mural installation, Cranbrook Academy of Art Museum, Bloomfield Hills, MI. Painted outdoor mural at Necker Children's Hospital, Paris.
1989	Campaigned World-wide for Aids awareness. Opened Pop Shop, Tokyo. Established Keith Haring Foundation.
1990	Painted BMW Automomible in Düsseldorf, Germany (BMW Collection).
1990	d. New York City, New York.

ANDY MOUSE I

ANDY MOUSE II

PREVIOUS TWO PAGES: "BEST BUDDIES©" WITH NEW YORK STREET FOOD; "CHICKEN CHILI AND ONION SAUTE"

© 1985 THE ESTATE OF KEITH HARING

△

CHICKEN CHILI

serves 8-10

2 pounds chicken breast,
small dice

---

1 pound cooked kidney beans

1-12 ounce can Mexican
stewed tomatoes

---

2 tablespoons chili powder

---

1 tablespoon ground cumin

---

1 tablespoon fresh chopped garlic

---

1 medium onion, small dice

1-4 ounce can diced green chile

---

1 cup of your favorite BBQ sauce

1-10 3/4 ounce can cheddar
cheese soup

---

1 small can tomato sauce

---

2 tablespoons olive oil

Tabasco sauce to taste

In a heavy-bottomed non-reactive sauce pot heat the olive oil over medium-high heat. Add chicken, cook until golden brown. Add onion and garlic. Sauté until translucent. Add remaining ingredients. Bring to a simmer. Cook for 45 minutes. Serve with your favorite hot dog. You can also garnish hot dogs with whole grain mustard, sauerkraut, or sautéed red pepper and onion. The New York Street way.

Boulevard Pale Ale, Kansas City, Missouri

ANDY MOUSE III

ANDY MOUSE IV

© 1985 THE ESTATE OF KEITH HARING

ABOVE: "AMULETIC BEADS #1 (GOLD AND SILVER CLOISONNÉ ENAMEL) AND "NINE SKETCHES #VI-PISTACHIO" BROACH
(GOLD AND SLIVER CLOISONNÉ ENAMEL ON COPPER; 14K, 24K GOLD, STERLING SILVER, TOURMALINE, PEARL) OPPOSITE:
JIM'S LAPEL PIN (GOLD AND SILVER CLOISONNÉ ENAMEL AND COURTNEY'S BABY TOOTH) WITH "CURRY RIVA" AND "SWEET ROYAL RICE

"There is magic in the unknown…I attempt to make objects of the unknown."

1944	b. Bucyrus, Ohio.
1966	Received Bachelor of Science degree from Western Reserve University.
1967	Received Masters in Science degree, Western Reserve University, also Certificate, Cleveland Institute of Art, OH.
1972	Received Horace E. Potter Award for Craftsmanship at Cleveland Museum of Art, OH.
1974	Received Craftsmanship Research Fellowship from the National Endowment of the Arts.
1977	Exhibition, "William Harper: Recent Works in Enamel" Renwick Gallery of the National Collection of Fine Arts Smithsonian Institution, Washington, D.C.
1977	Created "Pagan Baby" series using hair, snake rattles, snail and sea creature shells.
1978	Traveled to London, Spain, and Morocco. Exhibition, "The Vatican Museum," Vatican City, Italy.
1980	Completed "Nine Sketches" series.
1982	Commissioned to create the "Yale Collar" and "Yale Jewel for the Office of President."
1985	Exhibition, "Victoria and Albert Museum," London, England.
1988	Delivered lecture at Beinnale International, L'Art de L'Email, Limoges, France.
1990	Exhibition, "American Craft Museum," WILLIAM HARPER: ARTIST AS ALCHEMIST, (Orlando Museum of Art, Orlando, FL).
1994	Created "Jasper's Variations and Fabergé's Seeds."
1996	Exhibition, "Peter Joseph Gallery," "Ear Follies," NYC.
1998	Lives with his wife Riva in New York City, New York.

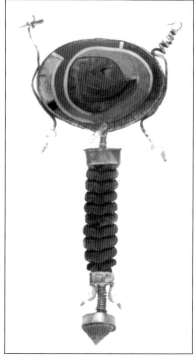

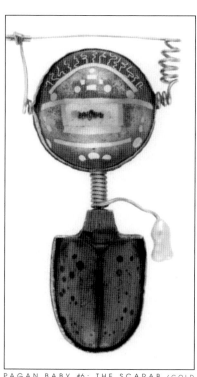

PAGAN BABY #4: THE SERPENT (SILVER/GOLD CLOISONNÉ ENAMEL ON COPPER, STERLING SLIVER, FRESH AND SALT WATER PEARLS, SHELL, AND SNAKE RATTLE

PAGAN BABY #6: THE SCARAB (GOLD CLOISONNÉ ENAMEL ON SILVER, 14K, 18K, AND 24K GOLD; STERLING SILVER; SHELL; FRESH WATER PEARL AND INSECT SHELL)

CURRY RIVA
Serves 10 - 12

The Meat:

2 pounds shrimp, about 30 large, peeled and deveined

2 pounds skinless chicken breasts, cut into thin strips

The Curry Paste:

1/2 cup finely chopped shallots

2 large onions, coarsely chopped

1/2 cup garlic, chopped and minced

4 tablespoons lemon grass, chopped, or
2 tablespoons grated lemon rind

4 tablespoons fresh ginger, chopped

2 tablespoons jalapeño pepper, chopped

2 tins anchovy fillets

2 teaspoons salt

2 tablespoons olive oil

1 teaspoon dried red pepper flakes

1 tablespoon cumin seeds

1 tablespoon dried coriander seeds

1 teaspoon ground nutmeg

1 teaspoon ground turmeric

1 teaspoon garam masala

1 stick cinnamon

1/2 cup honey

1/2 cup molasses

2 bunches fresh coriander (cilantro)
Combine these nineteen ingredients in a blender to make a thick curry paste. Set aside.

The Vegetables:

3-4 sweet peppers (red, green and yellow if possible)

1/2 lb fresh snow peas

1/2 lb baby carrots, blanched

3 tablespoons olive oil

3/4 cup grated coconut, soaked in enough water to just cover

Core the pepper, then cut into strips 1/2 inch wide. Heat the olive oil in a sauce pan or wok, and when hot, stir-fry the vegetables until medium soft, not more than 10 minutes. Add the chicken strips and continue cooking five minutes. Finally, add shrimp and cook until they turn pink. Add coconut then curry paste mixture and bring to a boil. If thinning is needed, add a good quality chicken stock until desired consistency is reached.

SWEET ROYAL RICE
Serves 10 - 12

3 to 4 tablespoons olive oil

2 large onions, finely chopped

1/4 cup garlic, finely chopped

4 cups basmati rice

1 tablespoon ground coriander

2 cinnamon sticks, broken into pieces

6 whole cloves

1/2 teaspoon nutmeg

9 cups rich chicken stock

2 teaspoon salt

1/2 cup dark brown sugar

2/3 cup molasses

2/3 cup dark raisins

2/3 cup golden raisins

Over a medium flame, heat the oil in a large heavy-bottomed pot (with a tight fitting lid to be used later). When very hot, add the onions and garlic.

Immediately lower heat so as not to burn, and cook on medium heat, stirring occasionally until golden, almost caramelized.

Add rice and spices and stir constantly over medium heat for about two minutes.

Add stock, brown sugar, molasses, salt, and raisins. Cook very low, with cover, about 40 minutes, until liquid is entirely absorbed.

Note: For extra special occasions, the rice may be covered with pure silver or gold leaf after placed in serving dish.

JOSH'S LONG ISLAND ICED TEA

1 jigger Absolut Citron® vodka

1 jigger Beefeater® gin

1 jigger Bacardi® light rum

1 jigger sour mix

Dash of Coca Cola®

Mix ingredients and serve in a tall iced glass with a wedge of lemon. If desired, a more "traditional" iced tea includes 1 jigger Triple Sec.

RATTLE FOR A WHITE WITCH
(GOLD AND SILVER CLOISONNÉ ENAMEL ON COPPER, ELECTRO-
FORMED COPPER, MIRROR, PEBBLES AND CAST SILVER-BRONZE)

ABOVE: "I'M HERE, I'M HERE, I'M HERE" BELOW: "THE END OF INNOCENCE" OPPOSITE: "THE EMBRACE" (PHANTOM OF THE OPERA)
WITH "OSSOBUCO ALLA MILANESE AND TRUFFLED MASHED POTATOES" ON FRANK LLOYD WRIGHT'S "IMPERIAL CHINA" BY TIFFANY & CO.

"Rose is the most beautiful thing in my life — she's always there, my backdrop and my audience, a constant source of amusement and inspiration."

1938	b. Easton, Connecticut.
1956	Studied art through correspondence.
1957	Married Rose.
1979	Solo exhibition, American Illustrators Gallery, Atlanta, GA.
1981	Exhibited art at the Smithsonian Institute, Washington, D.C.
1982	Solo Exhibition, Vineyard Gallery, Dallas, TX.
1984	Solo Exhibition, The Stable Gallery, London, England.
1985	Solo Exhibition, Royal Opera House, Covent Garden, London, England.
1986	Established the "Obsession of Dance Company" (the interpretation of dance and ballet through art).
1986	Solo exhibition, Royal Festival Hall, London, England. Opened by Princess Margaret.
1987	Painted original casts of both "Phantom of the Opera (London, England) and "CATS" (London, England).
1987	Solo Exhibition, Hotel de Paris, Monte Carlo, opened by Princess Caroline of Monaco.
1988	Designed set for "The Garden of Eros" for the London City Ballet.
1990	Solo Exhibition, Royal Academy of Dancing and Royal Opera House, London, England.
1993	Completed paintings and drawings of the "Still Life at the Penguin Cafe Ballet."
1995	Painted David Bintley's cast of "The Dance House" including designs of the costumes and sets for the San Francisco Ballet Company.
1996	Traveled to Tokyo, Japan to paint the theatrical forms of the Noh Theatre of Japan.
1998	Lives with wife Rose in a 300 year old farm house in Connecticut.

"STILL LIFE AT THE PENGUIN CAFE BALLET"

"OSSOBUCO ALLA MILANESE" BRAISED SHIN OF VEAL
Serves 4

4 veal shanks, including marrow bone

flour for dusting

2 tablespoons butter with 1 teaspoon olive oil

1/2 cup dry white wine

8 ounces tomatoes, peeled and chopped

meat stock or water, approximately 6 to 8 cups

salt and pepper to taste

For the Gremolada:

4 tablespoons parsley, finely chopped

1 tablespoon lemon rind, finely grated

1 small clove garlic, crushed

1 anchovy, finely chopped (optional)

Coat meat with flour, in a heavy saucepan brown in butter and oil on both sides. Add the wine, simmer for 10 minutes, add the tomatoes, stock or water to cover completely. Season with salt and pepper. Cover, simmer for 1 1/2 to 2 hours, stirring occasionally to make sure it does not stick, until the meat is tender and falling away from the bone. Sauce should be thick after cooking. Prepare the gremolada by mixing together all ingredients. Garnish each shank before serving.

Opus One 1993, Napa Valley, California

ROSALIE'S CHEESECAKE

For the Crust:

1 3/4 cups graham cracker crumbs (about 26 crackers rolled fine)

3/4 cup butter, melted

1 tablespoon brown sugar

For the Filling:

24 ounces cream cheese

4 eggs

1 cup sugar

1 teaspoon vanilla

For the Topping:

1 pint sour cream

3/4 cup sugar

Preheat oven to 400° F. Prepare the crust by mixing together the crumbs, melted butter and sugar and pressing onto the bottom of a 9 in. spring form pan. Set aside. In a mixing bowl, combine cream cheese, eggs, sugar and vanilla and beat at medium speed for 20 to 25 seconds. Pour cheese mixture in the spring form pan. Bake for 10 minutes, watching carefully. It should brown very slightly on top. Refrigerate at least over night and don't count the calories!

TRUFFLED POTATOES
Serves 4-6

6 medium Idaho potatoes

1 stick butter, cubed

3 tablespoons white truffle oil (can be found in specialty food markets)

salt and black pepper

white or black truffle shavings

Place quartered potatoes in heavy-bottomed, non-reactive sauce pot. Cover with cold salted water and bring to a boil. Simmer until potatoes are tender. Drain water and return to low heat until potatoes have dried, approximately 2 minutes. Add butter, season with salt and pepper to taste. Mix with a potato masher to desired consistancy. Mix in truffle oil. Serve topped with black truffle shavings.

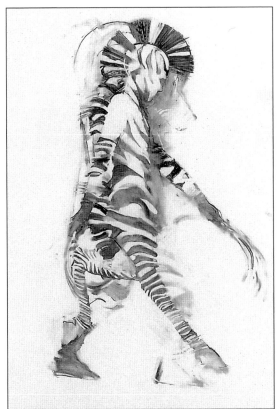

"STILL LIFE AT THE PENGUIN CAFE BALLET"

"I like to play with an idea, then watch it grow."

1914	b. near Apache, Oklahoma. Father an English translator for Geronimo.
1934	Studied under Dorothy Dunn at the Santa Fe Indian School.
1936	Exhibits paintings at the World's Fair, NYC.
1940	Studied with Norwegian muralist Olle Nordmark at Fort Sill Indian School in Anadarko, OK.
1941	Worked as a pipe fitter in Los Angeles during World War II while painting.
1948	Commissioned to create memorial sculpture "Comrade in Mourning."
1949	Won Grand Award at Philbrook Art Center, Tulsa, OK.
1954	Received French government's Palmes d'Acadèmique Award.
1968	First bronze casting at Nambè in Pojoaque, NM.
1971	Exhibition, Philbrook Art Center, Tulsa, OK.
1976	PBS documentary "Allan Houser: Working Sculptor."
1977	Commission, "Coming of Age" for Denver Art Museum.
1981	Exhibition, Grand Palais, Paris.
1983	Opens touring exhibition at Amerika Haus, Berlin.
1984	Exhibition, Kunstlerhaus, Vienna.
1985	"Offering of the Sacred Pipe" for the United Nations, NY.
1986	Dedicates "The Future" for Cavan Associate, Albuquerque, NM.
1986	"Bronze Bust of Geronimo" to Fort Sill Apache Tribal Center in Apache, Oklahoma, presented by President Bush.
1992	Awarded the "National Medal of the Arts" by the National Endowment of the Arts.
1993	Winner Prix de West for "Smoke Signal" National Cowboy Hall of Fame, Oklahoma City, OK.
1996	d. Santa Fe, New Mexico.

The following was written by Allan Houser's (Haozous) mother, Blossom Wratten Haozous. Blossom Haozous was born an Apache prisoner of war in Alabama in 1893 and moved with her family to Fort Sill, Oklahoma one year later. The excerpt is from WOMEN OF THE APACHE NATION, by H. Henrietta Stockel and describes the simple foods that young Allan Houser was raised on and loved.

"In speaking of how life was while they were still at Fort Sill, Mrs. Haozous described the way the women made bread. 'It was what people call tortillas now,' she said. 'They flatten it (the dough) out and cook it over the hot coals. They didn't have a grill to cook it on. They made a little rack and put live coals under it. You browned one side and then turned it over and browned the other. They made a rough rack out of bailin' wire mostly. Wove it back and forth and then put little legs on 'em or propped it on rocks to hold it up. The bread would rise a little bit and make bubbles. They'd have big baskets of bread like that to give out to the people with meat and corn, and sometimes they would use dried fruit like peaches . . . We dried pumpkin, too. You cut the pumpkin open and dug out all the seeds and then you peeled it. . . Then you start cuttin' around and just make a long string of it. . . then you drape 'em over a line . . . or branches and let 'em dry.'"

After her marriage, she attended a group meeting in which a demonstration agent taught her how to can and do a lot more cooking. She first canned green beans, and then corn.

"We didn't have no pressure cookers and we just had to boil 'em in a big kettle. Jars and all. That's the way she taught us to can."

"We just had fryers once a year during spring. When our fryers came in, why we killed 'em and we fried 'em like we were gonna eat them, then we put 'em in a jar and processed 'em. . . She taught us how to can chicken. And beef the same way. We'd cook the beef, then put it in jars, put liquid in it, then processed it . . . It's been years since I canned . . . We still like our dried meat. I don't dry much anymore, but once in a while I get a piece of steak and tenderize it, beat it, then put it out to dry."

– Blossom Haozous
(Allan's Mother)

PREVIOUS TWO PAGES; FIRST, "SACRED RAIN ARROW" SECOND: "FRIENDLY TALK" WITH "SQUASH BLOSSOM OMELET, BEEF JERKY AND INDIAN CHICK PEAS" ON 1890 LAKOTA BEADED VEST

SQUASH BLOSSOM OMELET
serves 4

8 eggs, beaten

---

8 fresh squash blossoms, stems removed, 4 roughly chopped

---

2 ripe tomatoes, diced

---

2 tablespoons fresh cilantro, chopped

1/2 cup grated monterey jack cheese

---

salt and pepper to taste

---

2 tablespoons butter

In a non-stick egg skillet, melt the butter over medium-high heat. Add the eggs, chopped squash blossoms, tomatoes, cilantro, and salt and pepper to taste.

Stir constantly with a rubber spatula until eggs begin to set. When setting begins, stop stirring and add the cheese.

Run the spatula around the edge of the omlet to loosen.

Fold into thirds. Serve on warm plates and garnish with whole squash blossoms, Apache chick peas and beef jerky if desired.

APACHE CHICK PEAS
serves 6-8

2 cups dried chick peas (garbanzos)

---

1 1/2 quarts water

---

2 teaspoons salt

1/4 cup butter

---

2 onions, minced

1/2 teaspoon dried hot red peppers

---

2 tomatoes, peeled and chopped

---

1 1/2 cups beef bouillon

Soak the peas overnight in the water with the salt. Bring the peas to a boil. Reduce the heat and simmer until almost tender, about 30 minutes. Drain, reserving the liquid. In a skillet heat the butter. Add the onion and cook until transparent. Add the seasonings and tomatoes and cook 10 minutes. Add to the peas. Add the bouillon and enough of the liquid (in which the peas were cooked) to cover the mixture. Cover and simmer 20 minutes.

Fresh "Squeezed" Watermelon Juice

CKWISE FROM UPPER LEFT: "CHOCOLATE CAKE, CREME BRULEE, BANANA CAKE, AND STRAWBERRY ICE" WITH "CARLO MORETTI GLASSES"
ATO SALAD," "GRILLED POLENTA," "CHEESE GRITS," "PESTO CRUSTED LAMB" AT JAMES AT THE MILL RESTAURANT AND INN AT THE M

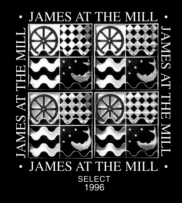

• JAMES AT THE MILL •

JAMES AT THE MILL

JAMES AT THE MILL

• JAMES AT THE MILL •

SELECT
1996

CALIFORNIA

CHARDONNAY

• JAMES AT THE MILL •

JAMES AT THE MILL

JAMES AT THE MILL

• JAMES AT THE MILL •

SELECT
1995

CALIFORNIA

CABERNET SAUVIGNON

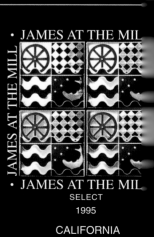

• JAMES AT THE MILL •

JAMES AT THE MILL

JAMES AT THE MIL

• JAMES AT THE MIL •

SELECT
1995

CALIFORNIA

ZINFANDEL

"To me, cooking is the ultimate art form. When it all comes together — the sounds of searing meats and poping wine corks hover like mist in the valley — it's quite a rush!"

1968	b. Savannah, Georgia, mother a speech pathologist.
1987	Studied Architecture at the University of Arkansas, Fayetteville, AR.
1989	Interned at American Seasons Restaurant and Something Natural (Bakery) and worked on Fishing Boats in Nantucket, MA.
1990	Received AOS degree from New England Culinary Institute (NECI) in Monpelier, VT.
1991	Joined Chef David Burke's opening crew at "Park Avenue Cafe," NYC.
1992	Became a sous chef for Chef Don Pintabona at Tribeca Grill, NYC. Worked for Chef Guy Savoy at "Guy Savoy" Restaurant, Paris. Worked at Sir Richard Rogers' "River Cafe" with Chef Rose Gray, and Ruth Rogers, London. Studied at the International School of Confectionery Arts, Washington, DC.
1993	Became a line cook for Chef Mark Miller at "The Coyote Cafe," Santa Fe, NM. Assisted in the production of CHEF MARK MILLER'S SALSA BOOK.
1994	Married Courtney Talbot Lambeth, Miami, FL.
1995	Opened "James at the Mill Restaurant," Fayetteville, AR. Created "Ozark Plateau Cuisine.™" Guest chef at the Justin Vineyards, Paso Robles, CA.
1996	Guest chef at the James Beard Foundation, NYC. Guest chef at the Hotel Paradis, Mauritius Island, Indian Ocean.
1997	Chosen to be on PBS "America's Star Chefs" series. Developed a gourmet food line "James at the Mill™" for Sams Club International, and is consultant for Tyson Foods International.
1998	Lives with wife Courtney in Fayetteville, Arkansas, and Miami, Florida.

• •

CREAMY WAR EAGLE MILL GARLIC CHEESE GRITS WITH CHILE SEARED SHRIMP AND PARMESAN TUILLE
Serves 4-6

5 cups chicken stock

2 cups stone ground corn grits

1 cup parmesan cheese

2 tablespoons chopped garlic

1 tablespoon fresh chopped parlsey

1 tablespoon fresh chopped chives

salt and pepper

For corn grits:
In a heavy bottom sauce pot, toast garlic in approximately 2 tablespoons butter until golden brown. Add chicken stock, salt and pepper and bring to a boil. Whisk in corn grits, cover and cook until grits are tender. Once the grits are tender fold in the parmesan cheese, fresh herbs and check seasonings. Save a little of the fresh herbs for garnish.

For the parmesan tuille:
Place grated parmesan cheese on a non stick baking sheet in 2-inch diameter circles using a cookie or biscuit cutter. Place in a preheated 400ºF oven and bake until golden brown.

For the shrimp:

4 tablespoons chile oil

8-12 large shrimp, peeled and deveined

salt

ground fresh black pepper

In a heavy bottom sauté pan heat the chile oil until hot. Sear the shrimp until pink and cooked through, but not over done. Season with salt and pepper and serve immediately.

To Assemble:
Layer the grits in between the parmesan tuilles and garnish with the shrimp and fresh chopped herbs.

> James At The Mill Select Chardonnay 1996, Napa Valley, California

SPICED RACK OF PORK WITH GARLIC CHEESE GRITS AND GRANNY APPLE CHUTNEY
Serves 4-6

For the pork and pork brine:

4 pounds bone-in pork loin, cut into 4-6 equal portions

1 quart cold water

1 cup brown sugar

1 tablespoon coriander seed

4 star anise

2 cinnamon sticks

In a heavy bottom non-reactive sauce pot combine the water, brown sugar, corriander seed, star anise and cinnamon sticks. Bring to a boil. Once the brine boils, remove from heat and let steep for 30 minutes, then cool. Once the brine is cool, place the portioned pork loin in the brine and marinate for 24 hours. The next day, remove the pork from the brine, pat dry and discard the brine. Grill or roast the pork to desired doneness, serve with creamy grits and apple chutney.

For the grits:

5 cups chicken stock

2 tablespoons butter

2 cups stone-ground corn grits

1 cup parmesan cheese

2 tablespoons fresh chopped garlic

1 tablespoon fresh chopped parsley

1 tablespoon fresh chopped chives

salt and pepper to taste

In heavy bottom sauce pot, toast garlic in approximately 2 tablespoons butter until golden brown. Add chicken stock, salt and pepper and bring to boil.

Whisk in corn grits. Reduce heat to medium, cover and cook until grits are soft. Fold in parmesan cheese and fresh herbs. Season with salt and pepper.

For apple chutney:

1/2 cup honey

10 Granny Smith apples, small dice

1 large white onion, small dice

1 cup dried apricot, julienne slice

1 lime, zest and juice

1 orange, zest and juice

2 Earl Grey tea bags

1 vanilla bean, split and scraped (save husk)

3 tablespoons dried thyme

In heavy bottom sauce pot, caramelize honey. Reduce heat to medium. Add citrus juice, cook until juice is almost evaporated.

Add onions, scraped vanilla beans and husks of vanilla beans. Cook until soft.

Add zest, apricot and tea bags. Cook an additional 3-4 minutes.

Fold in apples and dried thyme, remove from heat and let steep for 30 minutes. Remove bean husks and tea bags, stretch on a cookie sheet, cool and serve.

James At The Mill Select Cabernet Sauvignon 1995, Napa Valley, California

PESTO CRUSTED RACK OF LAMB ON WILD MUSHROOM POTATO HASH
Serves 4-6

For the pesto:

1/2 pound fresh spinach leaves

1/4 ounce fresh basil leaves

1 1/2 tablespoons fresh chopped garlic

8 ounces fresh pine nuts

8 ounces fresh grated parmesan cheese

1 teaspoon salt

1 teaspoon fresh ground black pepper

Place all the ingredients in a food processor and purée, occasionally scraping down the sides with a rubber spatula, until smooth.

Remove and place in an air-tight container. Refrigerate until needed. This pesto will keep for up to two weeks under refrigeration and freezes well also.

For wild mushroom potato hash:

3 pounds russet potatoes, peeled, medium dice

6 ounces shiitake mushrooms, stems removed, medium dice

6 ounces portobello mushrooms, stem removed, medium dice

6 ounces oyster mushrooms, stems removed, medium dice

2 large white onions, small dice

2 red bell peppers, small dice

1/4 cup fresh thyme, picked and chopped

2 cups heavy cream

salt

fresh ground black pepper

butter

corn oil

In a large heavy bottom sauté pan heat the corn oil until hot, add the potatoes. Cook over medium high heat until golden brown.

Remove the browned potatoes using a slotted spoon onto a paper towel and season with salt, reserve until later. Using the same pan add remaining ingredients, sauté until hot throughout.

Add the fresh thyme and cream, season with salt and pepper, bring the cream to a boil and simmer for 5 minutes.

Add the reserved potatoes and heat through. Serve immediately.

For rack of lamb:

2 racks of lamb, frenched

corn oil

salt

fresh ground black pepper

Season the lamb with salt and pepper to taste, sear in a heavy bottom sauté pan in 2-3 tablespoons of corn oil until golden brown.

Finish roasting the lamb in a pre-heated 400ºF oven to desired temperature.

I like to serve lamb medium rare and this typically takes 6 to 8 minutes in the pre-heated oven.

Once the lamb is done to desired temperature, remove from the oven and let rest at room temperature for 2 to 3 minutes.

After resting spread the pesto on the lamb, covering the loin 1/4 inch in thickness.

Flash the lamb in the oven for 1-2 minutes, to heat the pesto.

Then slice into equal portions and serve immediately with the wild mushroom potato hash and reduced veal stock.

Recipes continued on pages 226

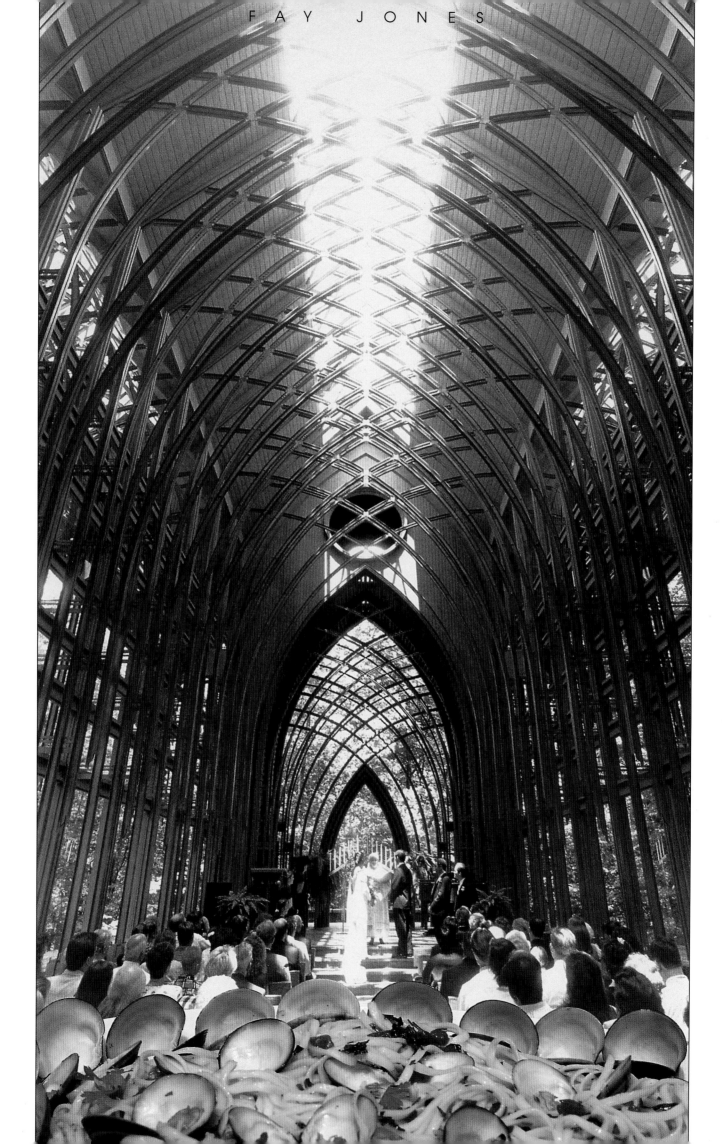

"We have the power and responsibility to shape new forms in the landscape - physical and spatial forms that will nourish and express that all-important intangible of the human condition at its spiritual best."

1921	b. Pine Bluff, Arkansas.
1941	Became a Navy Pilot in World War II.
1943	Married Gus (Mary Elizabeth Knox).
1950	Bachelor of Architecture, University of Arkansas, Fayetteville, AR.
1951	Masters in Architecture, Rice University, Houston, TX.
1951	Taught at University of Oklahoma with Bruce Goff, Norman, OK.
1953	Taliesin Fellowship, Apprenticeship to Frank Lloyd Wright, Spring Green, WS.
1964	"Orville Faubus Residence," Hunstville, AR.
1965	"Stone Flower" Shaheen Goodfellow Residence, Eden Isle, AR.
1976	Dean, School of Architecture, University of Arkansas, Fayetteville.
1980	"Thorn Crown Chapel," Eureka Springs, AR.
1981	Awarded "Rome Prize," (Prix di Roma), The American Academy in Rome.
1984	"Roy Reed House," Hogeye AR.
1988	"Cooper Memorial Chapel," Bella Vista, AR.
1989	"Worship Center," Eureka Springs, AR.
1990	American Institute of Architects Gold Medal presented by President Bush in White House, Washington, DC., attended by Prince Charles.
1992	FAY JONES by Robert Ivey, Jr., (A.I.A. Press, Washington, DC.).
1998	Lives with his wife Gus in Fayetteville, AR.

PREVIOUS TWO PAGES: FIRST: WEDDING AT "COOPER CHAPEL" BELLA VISTA, ARKANSAS WITH "PASTA WITH CLAMS"
SECOND: "THORNCROWN CHAPEL" EUREKA SPRINGS, AR ABOVE: ENTRY SCULPTURE, NELMS RESIDENCE, FAYETTEVILLE, AR

PASTA WITH CLAMS
serves 6

6 pounds clams
Little Neck or Manila
(small clams are preferred)

8 tablespoons extra virgin olive oil

1/2 cup dry white wine

3 garlic cloves, peeled and sliced

1 tablespoon hot
chile pepper flakes

12 ounces spaghetti

3 tablespoons fresh parsley,
chopped

1 small ripe tomato, peeled,
seeded and diced

salt and pepper

Scrub the clam shells, clean then soak in clean water, changing the water until it is clear. Put 3 quarts salted water in a large pot to boil. Heat 3 tablespoons olive oil in a large saucepan. Add 1/4 cup of the wine, half the chile flakes, and 1/2 the garlic. Add half the clams and cover with a lid, cooking on high heat until they open. Shake the pan constantly. When clams are open (discard the ones that don't open), remove entire contents of the pan and set aside (including juices).

Repeat the above process with the remaining clams and ingredients.

Prepare spaghetti, draining thoroughly. Mix pasta and clams well to coat the pasta. Add chopped parsley, diced tomato, salt and black pepper to taste.

Grgich Hills Fumé Blanc 1994,
Napa Valley, California

ENTRY SCULPTURE: FAY AND GUS JONES RESIDENCE FAYETTEVILLE, ARKANSAS

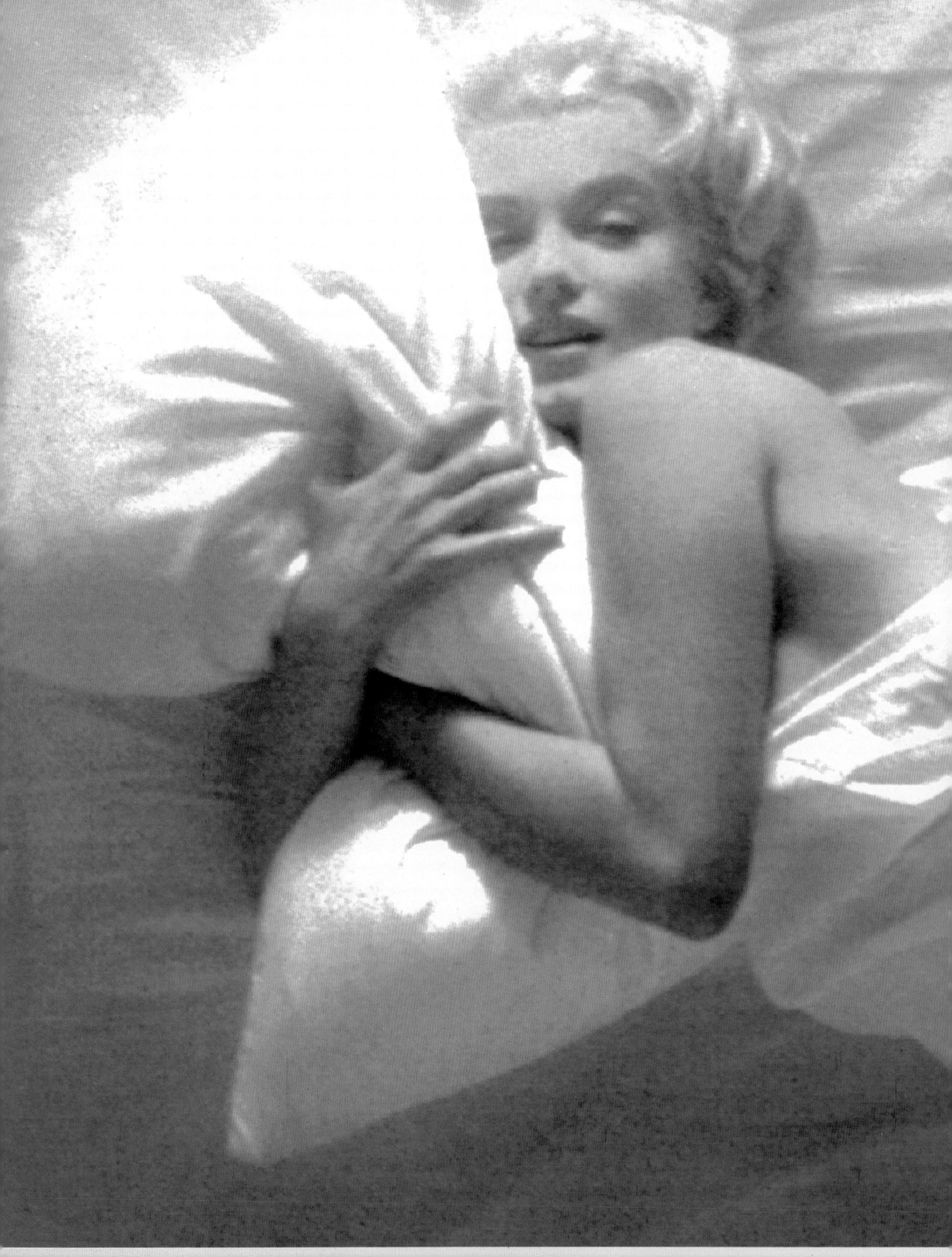

"I began seeing the world as a storehouse of images: gusts of snow, the red face of the minister, the river ice melting. Composing them, even mentally, gave me a feeling of competence I had never had. It was almost in fact, as if I became a different person."

1934	b. Toronto, father a tailor.
1944	Received his first camera, a Contax.
1949	Experimented with photography/took advanced photography course in NYC.
1958	Worked for Irving Penn NYC, Photographed Rogers/Hammerstein, NYC.
1959	Photographer for Popular Photography and Look Magazine.
1961	Photographed Marilyn Monroe, LA, CA, Elizabeth Taylor, Las Vegas, NV, Coco Channel, Paris.
1965	Protographed Brigitte Bardot, Mexico, Melina Mercouri, Rome, Burton /Taylor, Paris.
1966	Stanley Kubrick's photographer for film 2001: A SPACE ODYSSEY.
1969	Photographed Andy Warhol, Hollywood, CA; Ann-Margret, Las Vegas, NV.
1970	Photographed Francis Ford Coppola, San Francisco, CA; Catherine Deneuve, Vienna.
1971	Became photographer for Life Magazine.
1976	Photographed Farrah Fawcett (Same set-up as Marilyn Monroe, 1961)
1983	Photographed Dr. Stephen Hawking, Pasadena, CA, Orson Wells, Beverly Hills, CA.
1986	Photographed Grace Jones and Keith Haring at movie set of VAMP in Los Angeles. Haring painted Jones. Kirkland photographed in DAY IN THE LIFE OF AMERICA by De Moulin of Kodak.
1989	Published LIGHT YEARS, by Douglas Kirkland, (Thames and Hudson, Inc. NY).
1991	Began experiemnts with computer manipulation of images "digigraphs."
1993	Exhibited LIGHT YEARS at Berlin Amerika Haus, toured throughout Europe.
	Published ICONS, by Douglas Kirkland, (Collins, San Francisco).
1997	Published LEGENDS and BODY STORIES by Douglas Kirkland.
	Exhibited published photographs Scavi Scaligeri Gallery, Verona, Italy.
1998	Lives with his wife Françoise in Los Angeles.

· ·

TOURTE AUX LEGUMES
Serves 4-6

To make a Pate Brisse:

2 1/2 cups flour

2 sticks of cold butter, cut into small pieces

1 pinch salt

1/2 cup ice cold water

In the food processor or mixer add flour, butter and salt, mix for 30 seconds. Gradually add enough water to get the dough to stick together and finish making a ball by hand. Divide into two and let chill in the refrigerator for one hour. Unlike Martha Stewart, I prefer to get the dough back to room temperature before rolling it out thin. Butter half the dough. Pie dish should be about 2 inches deep and 8 to 9 inches in diameter. According to your mood you can mix herbs or spices to your dough, such as nutmeg, pepper, thyme, or fennel seed to enhance the taste of what you are going to fill it with.

To Prepare Vegetables:
Fill the pie to the edge with vegetables of your choice. The vegetables should be cooked al dente and drained from their water.

broccoli + ham + parmesan

artichoke hearts + roquefort + ham
ratatouille

peas + carrots +mushrooms + onions + asparagus, etc. in layers

spinach, mushrooms, sautéed pancetta

potatoes sliced + gruyere + onions

Add 2 or 3 eggs beaten with 4 tablespoons of creme fraiche, salt, pepper, whatever spices you are inspired by and cover with the other half of the rolled up pastry. Close the edges, rub an egg yolk over the top to get the golden color. Make a hole in the center, put a pie funnel or a piece of aluminum foil rolled up like a chiminey so the steam can escape and cook in a preheated oven at 375ºF for about three quarters of an hour, up to one hour.

FRANÇOISE'S SALAD
Serves 4-6

walnuts

avocado

pomegranate seeds

baby lettuce

orange with membrane removed

To Prepare Vinaigrette:
Whisk olive oil, balsamic vinegar,

salt, pepper, 1 teaspoon dijon mustard. Sauté walnuts in maple syrup till they are coated, assemble.

FRANÇOISE'S FRENCH PIZZAS
Serves 4

1 package puff pastry, thawed

1 tube Italian tomato paste (or 1 small can domestic paste)

2 tablespoons olive oil

1 pinch basil (dried)

1 pinch thyme (dried)

freshly grated parmesan

Various Suggested Toppings:
fresh tomatoes, seeded and grilled with olive oil

fresh basil grilled eggplant marinated in olive oil and garlic

grilled zucchini (courgette) and roasted yellow and red peppers marinated in olive oil and garlic

or all of the above

Prepare the crusts by brushing 4 sheets of the pastry with a mixture of the tomato paste, olive oil, basil, thyme, and sprinkle with parmesan. Bake until puffy and golden. Before serving, assemble the crusts with your choice of toppings. Place in a warm oven to reheat. Decorate with black pitted olives, fresh basil, springs of thyme and freshly grated parmesan.

Willamette Valley Whole Berry Pinot Noir 1996, Oregon

COCONUT CAKE

1/3 cup shortening

1 cup sugar

2 egg whites

1/2 teaspoon vanilla extract

2/3 cup coconut milk from a fresh coconut, save meat for icing

1 3/4 cup sifted all-purpose flour

2 teaspoons baking powder

1/2 teaspoon salt

Add all of the ingredients into a mixing bowl, beat at a medium speed for two minutes.

Pour into two 8-inch layer cake pans. Lined on the bottom with buttered wax paper. Bake in a preheated moderate oven 375ºF for 20 minutes. Cool, turn out on a rack. Remove the paper. Cover with the following frosting.

For the Frosting:

2 egg whites

1 1/2 cups sugar

1/8 teaspoon salt

1/3 cup milk

2 teaspoons light corn syrup

1/2 teaspoon vanilla extract

coconut from one fresh coconut

In the upper part of a double broiler combine all ingredients except vanilla and coconut. Put over boiling water, beat for 7 minutes or until frosting will stand in still peaks. Blend in vanilla. Frost the cooled cake. Add shavings from fresh coconut.

PHOTO FROM "BODY STORIES" © DOUGLAS KIRKLAND 1997

ABOVE: "MCKAMEY/JAMES RESIDENCE" FAYETTEVILLE, AR, WITH "PUFF PANCAKE" BELOW: "BERLIN WALL MEMORIAL AND CONFERENCE COMPLEX" MARSHFIELD, MO. OPPOSITE: "GARLIC SHRIMP/CHICKEN/FRENCH BREAD" WITH "SUNDANCING" AND "YOCUM SKI LODGE" SNOWMASS-AT-ASPEN, CO

86

SUNDANCING
THE ART AND ARCHITECTURE OF JAMES LAMBETH

"I remember now, lying on the lawn, burning secrets onto sycamore leaves with magnifying toys. Looking back, it seems I've always been playing cracker jack games with the sun."

1942	b. Kansas City, Missouri, Father and Mother residential developers.
1959	Pursued interest in industrial design at Los Angeles Art Center, School of Design. Made decision to study Architecture.
1966	Bachelor of Science and Bachelor of Architecture, Washington University, St. Louis, MO, Professors included Hans Hollein and Stanley Tigerman.
1967	Masters in Architecture, Rice University, Houston, TX.
1967	Married Joyce Talbot.
1968	Daughter Courtney was born.
1972	Began research in Passive Solar Design with 3 "Solar Modute Cabins" in the Ozark Mountains.
1972	"Best Architects Under 40" for "Combs Residence," by Architectural Record.
1973	"Yocum Ski Lodge," Snowmass-at-Aspen, CO, (First Focusing Arch. Lens to melt snow).
1975	"Delap Residence," Fayetteville, Arkansas. Determined by AIA Research Corporation to be the most efficient residence in U.S.A.
1976	"Excellence in Engineering" Award for Solar Lens of "Strawberry Fields Apartments," Springfield, MO, from the American Institute of Iron and Steel.
1977	SOLAR DESIGNING (privately published, Fayetteville, AR.) "Benjamin Spock Residence," Beaver Lake, AR.
1979	Awarded "Rome Prize," (Prix de Roma), American Academy in Rome.
1980	SOLAR 4, (Berlin: Amerika Haus) - also a traveling exhibition throughout Europe.
1981	Solar retrofit - "Ospedale dei Bambini," (Children's Hospital), Civitavecchia, Italy.
1983	"Desert Compound," Amargosa Desert, NV.
1985	Lectured throughout United States and Europe on Solar Design.
1993	SUNDANCING, (AIA press, Washington, D.C., and Miami Dog Press, Johnson, AR).
1994	"Inn at the Mill," (Clarion Inn of the Year 1995), Johnson, AR. Courtney married Chef Miles James, Miami, FL.
1995	"James at the Mill," Restaurant, Johnson, AR.
1998	Lives with his wife Joyce in Fayetteville, Arkansas and Miami, Florida.

SKETCHES FOR A CHILDREN'S BOOK "MA AND RA'S SOLAR ODYSSEY" 1979

THE ANNUNICATION

THE LAMAS

THE NECKLACE

THE DRAGON

AUTO

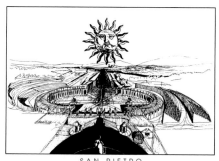

SAN PIETRO

BAR-B-QUE SHRIMP and/or CHICKEN
Serves 4

1 cup olive oil

1/2 teaspoon marjoram

1/2 teaspoon savory

2 teaspoons oregano

20 cloves garlic, not peeled

1/2 teaspoon thyme

3 teaspoons rosemary

2 teaspoons paprika

2 pounds shrimp, heads on

1-3 pounds chicken

1 lemon

salt and pepper to taste

Preheat oven to 300ºF. Wash shrimp and chicken well. Cut chicken into pieces, remove skin. Brown chicken in 1/4 cup olive oil. Add spices, herbs, garlic, lemon, remaining oil to chicken and bake for 30 minutes. Add shrimp, submerge in the oil and spices. Continue baking 30 minutes more, stirring occasionally. NOTE: You may double the amount of chicken and exclude the shrimp (or vice versa). Cook as above. Exclude the chicken browning step.

Stolichnaya Vodka, Club Soda with Lime Wedge

THE AMERICAN ACADEMY IN ROME

PUFF PANCAKE WITH STRAWBERRIES
Serves 4

2 eggs

1/2 cup milk

1/2 cup all-purpose flour

1/8 teaspoon nutmeg

1/4 cup butter

1/2 cup thinly sliced toasted almonds or hazelnuts

fresh lemon juice

3 tablespoons confectioners sugar

fresh strawberries, sliced and sweetened

In a food processor, add eggs, milk, flour, and nutmeg and blend until batter is smooth. Melt butter in 12-inch skillet until butter begins to foam. Stir in toasted almonds or hazelnuts. Add batter, covering the skillet evenly. Bake in 425ºF oven for 15-20 minutes or until golden brown. Sprinkle with lemon juice and return to oven for 2 minutes. Dust with confectioners sugar and serve with sweetened sliced strawberries.

LORENE'S FRIED APRICOT PIES

For the Crust:

2 1/2 cups all purpose flour

1/2 teaspoon salt

1/2 cup vegetable shortening, melted

1/2 teaspoon baking powder

1 1/2 tablespoon sugar

1/2 can canned cream or 3/4 cup half & half

For the Filling:

1 pound dried apricots

3/4 to 1 cup sugar

dash of salt

shortening for frying

For the crust, mix together all ingredients then separate into 2 rolls. Wrap tightly in wax paper, chill. Cover the dried apricots with water, cook until tender. Drain off most of the water, add salt and sugar. Cook until mashable. Cool. Roll out pastry dough into small saucer-sized rounds. Put about 2 teaspoons of fruit in the center of each round, fold over dough in a half moon shape. Seal the edges with a fork. Fry in hot shortening in a heavy cast iron skillet until browned evenly both sides. Drain on paper towels or brown paper bag (Illustrated p232).

SHADOW OF INNOCENCE

I SEE, I SEE

FLOWERS

TIME MACHINE

THE CAPTIVE

THE PAUSE

LICHTENSTEIN "CENTENNIAL MEDAL" FOR THE AMERICAN ACADEMY IN ROME   OPPOSITE: "ORECCHIETTE AL BROCCOLI DE RAPE"
ON "ELSA PERETTI'S CRYSTAL STAND" FOR TIFFANY & CO. WITH "LICHTENSTEIN: TAITTINGER COLLECTION CHAMPAGNE"

"I want my painting to look as if it were programed. I want to hide the record of my hand."

1923	b. New York City, father a realtor, mother a housewife.
1946	Received Bachelor of Fine Arts degree, Ohio State Univeristy, Columbus, OH.
1949	Received Masters in Art degree, Ohio State Univeristy, Columbus, OH.
	Studied at the Art Students League under Reginald Marsh, NYC.
1957	Solo Exhibition, John Heller Gallery, (Paintings Abastract Expressionism), NYC.
1962	Began "Pop Art," exhibited at Leo Gallery, LA., Galerie Sonnabend, Paris.
1964	Solo Exhibition, Leo Castelli Gallery, NYC.
1966	Exhibitied Cleveland Museum of Art, (Brush stroke paintings).
	"Standing Explosion," sculpture of enemeled metal.
1967	Began "Modern Paintings," series, exhibited at Indica Gallery, London.
1969	Solo Exhibition, The Guggenheim Museum, NYC.
1970	Solo Exhibition, The Galerie Sonnabend, Paris; Univeristy of Puerto Rico, PR.
	Exhibited at the Nelson Gallery of Art, Kansas City, MO.
1972	ROY LICHTENSTEIN by Diane Waldman (Harry N. Abrams, NY).
1974	Solo Exhibition, Galerie Mikro, Berlin.
1975	Solo Exhibition, Centre National d'Art Contemporain (Pompidou), Paris.
1977	Solo Exhibition, Manor Gallery, London.
1978	Solo Exhibition, Washington Gallery, Boston, MA.
1981	Solo Exhibition, The Whitny Museum, NYC.
1983	ROY LICHTENSTEIN by Lawrence Alloway (Abbeville, NY).
1984	Solo Exhibition, Leo Castelli Gallery, NYC.
1987	THE DRAWINGS OF ROY LICHTENSTEIN by Bernice Rose (MOMA, NY).
	as part of a Solo Exhibition at the Museum of Modern Art, NY.
1988	Received Honorary Doctor of Fine Arts degree, Ohio State University, Colubus, OH.
1989	"Resident Artist," The American Academy in Rome.
1992	Solo Exhibition, Galerie Ulysses, Vienna.
1993	ROY LICHTENSTEIN by Diane Waldman (Rizzoli, NY).
1996	Designed "Medal," for the American Academy in Rome.
1997	d. New York City.

ORECCHIETTE AL BROCCOLI DE RAPE
serves 4

1 pound broccoli rape

1/4 cup extra virgin olive oil

2 cloves minced garlic

1/4 cup dry white wine

1/2 teaspoon hot
red pepper flakes

1 pound orecchiette

salt

Trim broccoli rape of stems, etc and cut into 1-2 inch pieces and put into a large pot of boiling water. When the water returns to a boil remove the broccoli rape and plunge into ice water. Drain and put aside.

In the pot of boiling water add the one pound of orecchiette and cook (approximately 9-10 minutes). or until tender but firm. Drain well.

While pasta cooks, heat the oil in a large skillet over medium heat. Add the garlic and sauté until golden, careful not to burn. Add wine and reduce to half. Sprinkle in the pepper flakes and add broccoil rape and stir until completely coated with sauce. Add mixutre to cooked orecchiette, toss and serve immediately with grated parmesan cheese.

Taittinger Champagne 1985, Reims, France

"Every object which you pass from your hand must carry an outspoken mark of individuality, beauty and most exact execution."

1868	b. Glasgow, Scotland, father a police superintendent.
1884	Apprenticed to architect John Hutchison.
1889	Founded "The Four," with Herbert McNair, Margaret and Francis Macdonald.
1890	Won the "Alexander Thomsan Travelling Scholarship," traveled throughout France and Italy, drawing architectural monuments of the Renaissance.
1896	Won competition to design the new Glasgow School of Art. Designed two tea rooms for Miss Catherine Cranston in Glasgow - "Buchanan Street Tea Rooms," and Argyle Street Tea Rooms."
1900	Married artist Margaret Macdonald. Together they developed the "Glasgow Style." Their interior designs were introduced as a traveling exhibition that toured Veinna, Turin, Moscow, Dresden, Cologne, and Budapest. "Ingram Street Tea Rooms," Glasgow.
1901	"Windyhill House," Kilmacolm, Renfrewshire. "Daily Record Building," Glasgow. "House for an Art-Lover," competition.
1903	"Hill House," Helensburgh, Dunbartonshire. "Warndorfer Music Salon," Vienna, Austria.
1904	"Willow Tea Rooms," for Miss Catherine Cranston in Glasgow. Became a partner in the architecutal firm Honeyman and Keppie.
1906	"Scotland Street School," Glasgow. "Anchenibert House," Stirlingshire. "Mackintosh Residence," "Florentine Terrace," (reconstructed at Glasgow University, Museum of Art, Glasgow).
1911	"The White Cockade," an exhibition cafe for Miss Cranston for the 1911 International Exhibition in Glasgow.
1917	"Derngate Terrace House," Northhampton. The Mackintoshes moved to London.
1920	"Studio House," Chelsea, London (Mackitosh Residence).
1922	Designed textiles (free-lance).
1923	Abandonded architecture and moved to Port Vendres, France to establish a new career as a painter (completed Flower series).
1928	d. London.

MERINGUE SHELLS
serves 4

2 egg whites

1/2 cup ground hazelnuts

1/2 cup sugar

1/2 teaspoon vanilla extract

1/2 teaspoon cream of tartar

1/8 teaspoon salt

Add salt and cream of tartar to egg whites and beat until foamy. Add sugar gradually while beating eggs until mixture is stiff. Add vanilla, gently fold in hazelnuts. Spoon onto lightly buttered plain brown paper on cookie sheet and flatten to make a 2 inch square thin base. With a pastry tube surround base with mixture to create a square donut shape about 1" high. Bake in a preheated oven 275°F for 45 minutes, then reduce heat to 250°F and bake 15 minutes more until hard to the touch. Transfer shells to a damp board and then slowly remove from the paper. When cool, fill with ice cream, fruit or berry purée, fresh fruit or fresh berries and top with whipped cream. Garnish with candied flower blossoms.

Oban, 14 year old, West Highland, Scotland

CANDIED FLOWER BLOSSOMS
serves 4

Good flower petals to dry are roses, violets, and pansies (See page 203 for further suggestions).

In a bowl, combine one egg white and 3 or 4 drops of vodka and beat gently. Brush completely over each dried flower petal with egg white mixture. After egg coating; sprinkle sugar on petal until covered on both sides. Place the flower on waxed paper and allow to dry completely. If the room conditions are too humid for the flowers to dry overnight, then gently place them on a cookie sheet and put into the oven at 150°F - 200°F with the oven door open for two hours. Store the beautiful candied flowers in a sealed container.

"What is most important is the drive to create, which at times also gives us the hope of preserving the infinate. This is always the thought that accompanies our work, but it is a rare thing when the form preserves it."

1908	b. Bergamo, Italy, father was a shoemaker.
1921	Apprenticed as a wood sculptor carving angels for churches.
1919	Apprenticed in gilder's shop, making stucco friezes.
	Studied at the Accademialdi Belle Arti, Verona.
1927	Studied at the Academy of Fine Arts, Verona.
1930	Architect Muzio gave him his first commission for decorations for the Chapel of the Universita Cattolica del Sacro Cuore, Milan.
1933	Created "Young Girl on a Chair" in copper, Rome.
1936	Sculptures included in the Venice Biennale.
1938	Began a long series of bronze sculptures of Cardinals including an eight-foot image of Cardinal Giacomo Lercaro, Bologna.
1942	Taught at the Alberta Academy of Fine Arts, Turin.
1944	Was a partisan, hiding from the Germans.
1947	Exhibition of 50 bronzes and 100 drawings at the Palazzo Reale, Milan.
1948	Awarded Grand Prize for Italian Sculpture a the Venice Biennale. Sculpture included in exhibition at the Museum of Modern Art, NYC.
1950	Won an international competition by the Vatican to design reliefs for the fifth bronze door of St. Peter's Basilica "Doors of Death," installed 1964.
1956	Received commission to design the central portal of Salzburg Cathedral, Austria.
1964	Moved studio to Campo del Fico in Ardea (Near Rome).
1968	Installed bronze doors for the Church of St. Lawrence, Rotterdam.
1969	Solo Exhibition, "The Museum of Modern Art," NYC.
1970	Honorary Academician: Royal Academy of Arts, London.
1981	Italian Gold Medal of Merit, Rome, Le Muse Medal, Academy of the Muse, Florence.
1991	d. Rome.

ABOVE LEFT: HEDGEHOG (DETAIL, ST. PETER'S DOORS) ABOVE RIGHT: TURTLE (DETAIL, ST. PETER'S DOORS) PREVIOUS TWO PAGES: FIRST: ST. PETER'S BASILICA "DOOR OF DEATH" WITH SWISS GUARD SECOND: "PUTTANESCA PASTA" WITH LINCOLN FOX'S "DOVES"

SPAGHETTI ALLA PUTTANESCA
serves 2

16 large black olives, quartered

16 large green olives, quartered

2 tablespoons capers, chopped

3 cloves garlic, chopped

1/4 teaspoon Chinese chile paste, or other hot chile sauce

2 pounds tomatoes, peeled and chopped

1 teaspoon oregano, chopped

black pepper to taste

1/4 cup olive oil

5 whole small red chile pequin, or other small dried red chile

3 garlic cloves, slightly crushed

3 ounce anchovy filets, chopped

1/2 cup fresh parsley, chopped

3/4 pounds spaghetti

In a medium bowl, mix together olives, capers, chopped garlic, chile paste, tomatoes, oregano and black pepper. Set aside. Heat olive oil in a skillet and add dried chiles and crushed garlic. Cook until chiles are blackened and the garlic browned. Remove and discard the chiles and garlic. Add mixed ingredients and cook briskly for 20 minutes.

In a large stockpot, bring salted water to a boil. Cook pasta until al dente (a bit firm in the center). To the sauce, add anchovies and parsley. Lower heat and cook gently for about 3 minutes. Serve over hot pasta.

FRIED ARTICHOKES
serves 2

2 pounds baby artichokes, tops trimmed and tough outer leaves removed

1 lemon, squeezed

boiling salted water

1 tablespoon butter

1 tablespoon olive oil

In a large bowl, fill with water and lemon juice. Prepare the artichokes by scooping out the center, or chokes, and discard.

Place cleaned artichokes in lemon water to prevent turning black.

Blanch them in a saucepan of boiling salted water for about 2 minutes. Drain well. Cut the artichokes lengthwise into slices.

In a frying pan melt the butter and oil together over low heat. Add artichoke slices, cook covered for 5 minutes, stirring frequently. Sprinkle with salt, serve immediately.

> The Hess Collection, Napa Valley
> Cabernet Sauvingnon, 1994

COCONUT GELATO
(Ice Cream)
makes about 1 quart

1 - 15 ounce can sweetened cream of coconut

2 cups 2% milk

1 cup heavy cream

1/4 cup sweetened coconut flakes

1 cup hazelnuts or macadamia nuts, roughly chopped (optional)

Place the milk and coconut cream into a food processor and blend thoroughly.

Stir in the cream, nuts (optional) and coconut flakes. Pour the mixture into ice cream freezer and freeze. Enjoy!

WATERMELON SORBETTO
makes about 1 quart

1/2 medium watermelon

3/4 cup simple syrup (made by desolving equal parts of sugar into heated water then allowed to cool)

1 tablespoon fresh lemon juice

Remove rind and seeds from watermelon and purée in a food processor to make 3 cups juice. Stir in simple syrup and lemon juice to watermelon puree. Pour the mixture into ice cream freezer and freeze.

OWL (DETAIL, ST. PETER'S DOORS)

RAVEN (DETAIL, ST. PETER'S DOORS)

> "A lot of my work is related to childhood memory … and I think poetry is very important. I also think you can have fun and raise hell but I am always sensitive to courtesy. That's something that makes life nice."

1943	b. Memphis, Tennessee.
1960	Attended Memphis Academy of Arts and Southwestern College, TN.
1961	Opened his own clothing boutique in Memphis, TN.
1964	Solo exhibition of paintings, Cooper Gallery, NY.
1965	Received Scholarship to American Library in Paris, France. Moved to Paris, he studied at the Sorbonne and the Chambre. Syndicale de la Couture Parisienne, Paris.
1969	Assistant designer for Ted Lapidus, Paris.
1970	Designed movie set for "Diva" and "La lune dams le Caniveau."
1971	Designed collection for Jacques Heim, Paris (Haute Couture).
1973	Fur Collection for Neiman Marcus, Dallas, TX.
1974	Created the men's Collection for Yves Saint-Laurent.
1975	Designed sets and costumes for "Thomas," by Jean-Franças Dion.
1978	Gave a seminar on the theory of design, American Academy in Paris. Exhibited paintings at Sycamore Gallery, San Francisco, CA.
1979	Designed sets and costumes for "L'enfant roi," by Renè Feret.
1983	Won French Academy Award for best Art Direction for "La Lune dans le Caniveau."
1984	Directed commercials, the Johnny Halliday rock show and Busy's Video Clip "Adrian," which won several international awards.
1985	Designed Della Torre's first collection of porcelain for "Siècle."
1987	Created "Cactus" collection for Daum Crystal Works, Paris, now in the permanent collection of the Musée de Arts Dècoratifs, Paris, and the Corning Museum, NY.
1988	Designed first lamp collection for Drimmer (received the Oscar 88 Award). "Carnet de Voyage" for Hermès, also designed scarves and porcelain for Hermès, Paris.
1989	Designed the brand image for Charles Jourdan, Paris. "Parcours du Lin," Exhibition at Monte Carlo. Painted a fresco at the Chauèe d'Antin subway station, Paris. Image design for perfume "Amazone," for Hermès, Paris.
1990	HILTON MC CONNICO, edited by Michel Aveline (Memphis Brooks Museum, Memphis).
1994	Designed "Swatch Watches," "William Tell" collection for Daum.
1995	"Toupary Restaurant," La Samaritaine, Paris.
1996	Designed "Cheyenne Crystal," Daum.
1998	Lives in Paris, France.

PREVIOUS TWO PAGES: FIRST: "LOST ARROWS OF WILLIAM TELL" DESSERT PLATES AND DECANTER WITH "SPANISH SUN BURST" AND "PINK FINGERS" SECOND: "CACTUS" DESSERT PLATES, WINE GLASSES, AND DECANTERS, WITH "BISHOP'S ICED TEA" DESIGNS FOR DAUM, PARIS FRANCE

104

PINK FINGERS
serves 4

Take 2 chicories.

Clean them and cut off the end to obtain single straight leaves (no ugly leaves for this recipe).

Take a package of Philadelphia cream cheese.

Mix with 4 big spoons of sour cream, the juice of half a lemon, 18 drops of Tabasco sauce, 3 tablespoons of chopped chives.

Mix it all together with one spoon of vodka. Salt and pepper to taste.

Take the chicory leaves and spread the mixture in the hollow side of the leaf. Cover this with 3 small squares of smoked salmon and 3 "baies roses," (red peppercorns). Keep in the refrigerator one hour before serving.

SPANISH SUN BURST
serves 4

Take a pineapple and put it on a silver stand. On silver tooth picks, stab a round of very spicy chorizo.

Then put a ball of honeydew melon on the pick.

Take your picks and stick them in the pineapple to create a fireworks explosion look.

And that's all.

Be sure that the chorizo rounds are on the pineapple side.

THE BISHOP'S ICED TEA
serves 2

2 jiggers of Cognac

2 jiggers of Grand Marnier

3 jiggers of sweet cider

3 jiggers of cider brut

3 jiggers of iced tea

Leave it in the refrigerator 24 hours and just before serving add 3 jiggers of Champagne.

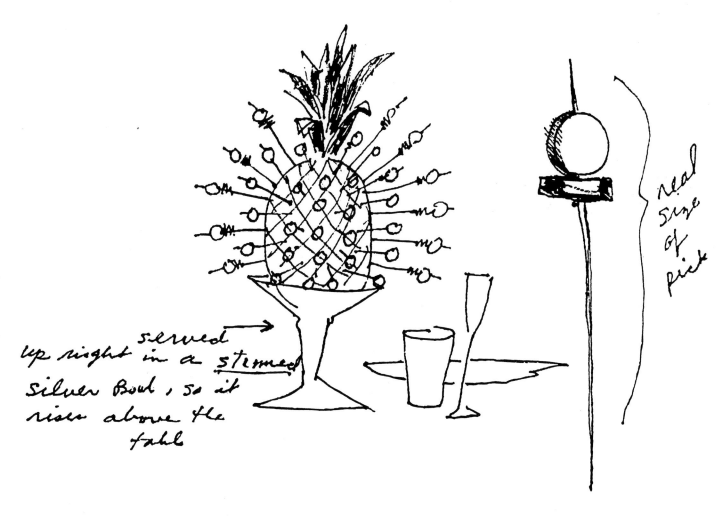

served up right in a stemmed Silver Bowl, so it rises above the table

real size of pick

"The white is always present but never the same, bright and rolling in the day, silver and effervescent under the full moon of New Year's Eve. Between the sea of consciousness and earth's vast materiality lies this ever-changing line of white. White is the light, the medium of understanding and transformative power."

1934	b. Newark, New Jersey.
1957	Received Bachelor of Architecture degree, Cornell University, Ithica, NY.
1960	Worked for Skidmore, Owings, and Merrill, NY.
1962	Worked for Marcel Breuer, NY. "Lambert Beach House," Fire Island, NY.
1965	"Stella Apartment," NY. "Jerome Meier Residence," Essex Fells, NJ.
1967	"Smith House," Darien, CN.
1969	"Staltzman House," East Hampton, NY. "Westbeth Artists' Housing," NYC., NY.
1972	Awarded the "Arnold Brunner Memorial Prize," by the National Institute of Arts and Lellers.
1973	"Douglas House," Harbor Springs, Michigan; "Shamberg House," Chappaqua, NY; "Twin Parks Northeast Housing," the Bronx, NY; "Museum of Modern Art at Villa Strozzi," Florence, Italy.
1975	"The Atheneum," New Harmony, IN. Exhibited "Architectural Studies and Projects," the Museum of Modern Art," NY.
1976	RICHARD MEIER, ARCHITECT by Kenneth Frampton (Warehouse Publications, NY.).
1980	Named "Officer de l'Ordre des Arts et des Letters." by the Ministry of Culture of France.
1984	Received "Pritzker Prize," for Architecture.
1985	Began "Getty Center," Los Angeles, CA; "Ackerberg House," Malibu, CA.
1988	Received "Royal Gold Medal," by the Royal Institute of British Architects. "Canal + Headquarters," Paris, France; "Museum of Contemporary Arts," Barcelona, Spain; "High Museum of Art," Atlanta, GA.
1990	Elected to the Belgian Royal Academy of Art. "Fox, Inc. Studio Expansion," Los Angeles, CA; "Aro Museum," Rolandswerth, Germany; "Swiss Volksbank," Switzerland; "Grange Road Medical Center," Singapore.
1991	RICHARD MEIER, ARCHITECT 2, by Kenneth Frampton and Joseph Rykwert, (Rizzoli International Publications, Inc. NYC.). "Office Building," Berlin, Germany. "Fabric Designs," for Design Tex; Received honorary doctorate from the University of Naples.
1997	Received "Gold Medal," The American Institute of Architects. "Getty Center," completed.
1998	Lives in New York City, New York and Los Angeles, California.

PREVIOUS TWO PAGES: "COCA-COLA® BBQ CHICKEN AND WATERMELON" AT THE "HIGH MUSEUM OF ART" ATLANTA, GA
BELOW AND OPPOSITE: "THE ATHENEUM," NEW HARMONY, IN

BBQ CHICKEN
serves 12

4 whole fresh chickens, cut into
individual pieces
- legs, thighs, wings, breasts

---

1 12-ounce can
or bottle Coca Cola®

---

1 large can frozen orange juice
concentrate (pineapple juice concentrate can be substituted
or you can use fresh
orange juice if you have it,
but frozen concentrate is best)

---

4 dashes Worcestershire sauce

---

8 dashes soy sauce

---

1 bottle ketchup,
or 1 bottle chili sauce, or both

---

1 teaspoon powdered ginger

1/2 teaspoon dried
red pepper flakes

1/2 teaspoon garlic salt
or 2 cloves fresh garlic, crushed

In a large shallow pan, combine cola, sauces and spices. Add chicken pieces skin side down and marinate for at least 1 hour, turning once.

Preheat charcoal grill.

Grill on barbecue for approximately 10 minutes per side, basting occasionally, or until crispy and well done.

Samuel Adams Boston Ale

"My chosen field of study - anthropology - led me to travel, and it dove-tailed perfectly with my culinary interest … Upon returning from these journeys, I would attempt to duplicate the dishes I had most recently experienced and try them on willing friends who shared my excitement for new taste sensations."

1949	b. Boston, Massachuttes.
1967	Studied Anthropology and Chinese Art History at U.C. Berkeley, Berkeley, CA. Met Jean Pierre Monllè, Paul Bertolli.
1976	Worked at Chez Panisse for Alice Waters in Berkeley, CA.
1979	Opened the Fourth Street Bar and Grill in Berkeley.
1980	Opened the Santa Fe Bar and Grill in Berkeley.
1987	Moved to Santa Fe and opened the Coyote Cafe, Santa Fe, NM.
1989	COYOTE CAFE by Mark Miller (Ten Speed Press, Berkeley, CA).
1990	Opened rooftop Cantina and Coyote Cafe General Store in Santa Fe, NM.
1992	Opened Red Sage Restaurant in Washington, D.C.
1993	COYOTE'S PANTRY by Mark Miller and Mark Kiffin, (Ten Speed Press, Berkeley, CA). Opened Coyote Cafe in Austin, TX.
1994	Opened Coyote Cafe in the MGM Grand Hotel, Las Vegas, NV. THE GREAT CHILE BOOK by Mark Miller, (Ten Speed Press, Berkeley, CA). Created "Raku Restaurants" specializing in Asian food, U.S. urban areas.
1995	MARK MILLER'S INDIAN MARKET COOKBOOK by Mark Miller, (Ten Speed Press, Berkeley, CA).
1996	FLAVORED BREADS FROM THE FAMOUS COYOTE CAFE by Mark Miller and Andrew MacLauchlan, (Ten Speed Press, Berkeley, CA).
1998	Lives in Washington, D.C. and Santa Fe, NM.

· ·

○
POSOLE
serves 6

6 pounds pigs' feet, cracked or cut

4 tablespoons whole Mexican oregano leaves

2 large white onions, sliced

6 bay leaves

2 large heads garlic, cut in half (across)

3 teaspoons black pepper

10 whole red chiles (mild to medium)

2 teaspoons cumin seed

1 teaspoon dried whole thyme

1 teaspoon salt

5 gallons water

2 pounds prepared posole (hominy corn)

2 pounds lean pork meat, diced

1/4 head green cabbage, thinly sliced

8 radishes, sliced

Simmer pig's feet, 2 tablespoons oregano, onions, bay leaves, one head garlic, pepper, chiles, cumin, thyme, and salt in the water for 6 to 8 hours, skimming often to remove excess fat and scum, especially during the first 2 hours. Strain and reserve stock. Add the posole, pork, remaining garlic, and 1 table-spoon oregano, to the strained stock, cover, and simmer until posole 'buds' open (at least 2 to 3 hours but up to 4 or 5 hours – actually the longer the better). Add more water periodically and skim regularly. Remove garlic and add

salt to taste if necessary. Ladle soup into bowls and garnish with shredded cabbage, radish sticks, red chile sauce, and remaining oregano. (The photograph on page 111 shows the Posole garnished with sautéed Purple Peruvian Potatoes.)

○
GRILLED SCALLOPS IN ORANGE AND SERRANO BROTH WITH GREEN PIPIAN
serves 4

For the Scallops:

24-32 large fresh sea scallops

4 cups water

4 teaspoons salt

2 tablespoons chile molido (ground red chile)

PREVIOUS TWO PAGES: FIRST, "GRILLED SCALLOPS," SECOND, "POSOLE"

4 tablespoons chopped cilantro

10 fresh serrano chiles, chopped with seeds

1/2 teaspoon ground black pepper

vegetable oil for grilling

For the broth:

2 cups orange juice

2 cups lobster stock

2 seranno chiles, blackened

1 tablespoon chopped black pepper

juice of 1 lime

salt to taste

For the pipian:

1/2 cup pumpkin seeds

1/4 cup diced onion

1 tablespoon peanut oil, plus 2 teaspoons

1/2 cup chicken stock

1/2 cup cilantro

4 leaves romine lettuce

3/4 teaspoon anise seed

1/2 teaspoon salt

1/2 teaspoon sugar

4 cloves roasted garlic

To prepare scallops, make a brine by stirring together the salt, molido, water, cilantro, pepper and serranos. Pour this mixture over the scallops, allow them to cure for 3-6 hours in the refrigerator. For the broth, combine all ingredients except the cilantro in a sauce pot and reduce over a slow simmer by 1/3 to 1/2 or until well flavored. Adjust the salt and lime levels to your taste, add the cilantro immediately prior to serving. When ready to make the pipian, dry roast the pumpkin seeds in a large sauté pan for about 5 minutes, stirrring often until they almost stop popping. Heat 1 tablespoon of the oil in a sauté pan, cook the onion over low heat until slightly browned. Purée the pumpkin seeds, onions and chicken stock together in either a

blender or food processor to form a paste. Add half of the cilantro and all of the remaining ingredients except the peanut oil and puree. Refry the pipian by heating the remaining oil almost to the smoke point in a sauté pan and adding the puree. Cook for 3-4 minutes, stirring constanly. Do not cook it for too long or it will take on an unappetizing gunmetal color. Allow the pipian to cool slightly, return it to the blender. Purée it with the remaining cilantro, hold it until ready to complete the dish. This sauce will keep, chilled, for up to 3 days, but it should be rewarmed slightly or be allowed to come up to room temperature before serving. Drain the scallops well. If desired, place them on skewers that have been soaked in water to facilitate easier grilling. If the scallops are exceptionally large, it may be necessary to use 2 skewers, side by side, to keep them from spinning when you try to turn them. Blot and oil the scallops slightly, grill for 2-3 minutes per side or until done to your taste. In the restaurant, we serve them medium rare or with translucent centers. Slide the scallops off of the skewers if using them, and divide evenly among 4 warm soup plates. Whisk the cilantro into the warm broth, pour it around the scallops. Top each scallop with a dollop of the pipian, serve at once with a good crusty bread.

Michel Niellon, Chassagne-Montrachet 1993, Burgundy, France

ROASTED LOIN OF PORK WITH FIG AND CHIPOTLE STUFFING
serves 4

For the Pork:

2 pounds boneless pork loin with the fat cap left on

1/4 cup molasses

1 1/2 cups orange juice

1 1/2 teaspoons chile caribe

1/2 cup rice vinegar

1 tablespoon olive oil

1 1/2 tablespoon chopped basil

1/2 cup tamarind purée, optional

olive oil to sear

For the Stuffing:

2 cups dried black mission figs, trimmed and roughly chopped

2 teaspoons thyme, chopped

2 tablespoons Italian flat leaf parsley, chopped

1/4 teaspoon salt

1 1/2 teaspoon roasted garlic, chopped

1 1/2 tablespoon lemon oil

1 teaspoon chipotles en adobo, puréed

1 teaspoon sherry or balsamic vinegar

1/4 cup pinenuts

To prepare the pork, blend together the orange juice, molasses, caribe, vinegar, oil, basil and pour it over the pork loin in a shallow pan. Allow the pork to marinate overnight. For the stuffing, place the figs, garlic and chipotles into a food processor, pulse unti semi-smooth. Transfer to a bowl, fold in the remaining ingredients, adjusting the quantities to your taste. Remove the pork from the marinade, blot dry. Reserve the marinade. Butterfly the loin, lengthwise, bookfold style. Leave 1/2 inch of meat to connect the two halves of the loin. Open the porkloin, cover it with plastic wrap. Pound it lightly with a butchers mallet or heavy pan until it is an even thickness, between 1/2-3/4 of an inch. Mound the stuffing down the center of the loin, fold it closed. Tie the loin carefully at 1 inch intervals with butchers string. The loin may be prepared to this point up to 24 hours in advance.

When ready to proceed, place the marinade into a sauce pot and reduce it at a slow simmer until a glaze-like consistency is achieved. Heat the olive oil, saute the loin over moderate heat to sear it. Transfer the pork to a roasting rack, roast in a preheated 325ºF oven for 40-50 minutes or until an internal temperature of 125º F is achieved. Carry over cooking will bring the center of the loin to a light rose color. Brush the pork liberally with the glaze during the last few minutes of cooking. Allow the loin to rest for 5 minutes or so before removing the twine and slicing. When ready to serve, slice the loin into 12 even slices and divide them among 4 warm serving plates.

ABOVE: "RED CUBE" MARINE MIDLAND BANK, NYC OPPOSITE: "SOFT SHELLED CRABS" ON "BIOMORPHIC COFFEE TABLE" FOR HERMAN MILLER

I S A M U   N O G U C H I

ARTIST

"It is my desire to view nature through nature's eyes."

1904	b. Los Angeles, California, father a poet, mother a teacher.
1906	Family moved to Tokyo.
1918	Sent alone to study in America.
1924	Entered Columbia Medical School, NYC.
	Decided against medical school and entered Leonardo da Vinci Art School, NY.
1927	Traveled to Paris on a Guggenheim Scholarship. Worked in Brancusis' Studio.
1928	Exhibited at the Eugene Schoen Gallery, NYC.
1935	Designed sets for Martha Graham's dance performances.
1938	Won first place in relief competition with stainless steel work, Rockefeller Center, NYC.
1943	"Visiting Artist," The American Academy in Rome.
1944	"Biomorphic Coffee Table," wood and glass, Herman Miller, Zeeland, MI.
1950	Received grant from Bollingen Foundation, traveled to Europe, Egypt, India and Japan. Exhibited at Mitsukosi Department Store, Japan.
1957	Designed Garden for Paris Unesco Building, France.
1960	Designed Marble Garden, Yale University, New Haven, CN.
	Designed Sculpture garden for Jerusalem National Museum, Israel.
1961	Established Long Island City Studio.
1968	Retrospective exhibition, Whitney Museum, NYC.
1970	Designed fountain for Expo '70, Osaka, Japan.
1973	Exhibited at Minami Gallery, Tokyo.
1974	Exhibited Guggenheim Museum, NYC, Designed fountain, Detroit Civic Center, MI.
1977	Designed fountain for Chicago Art Institute, Chicago, IL.
1978	Exhibited "Imaginary Landscapes," Walker Art Center, Minneapolis, MN.
1980	Created "Bay Front Park," Miami, FL.
1985	Presidents Medal, Washington, D.C.
	First comprehensive exhibition of "Akari Lamps," Art Forum, Tokyo.
	Opened Noguchi Garden Museum, Long Isalnd City, NY.
1986	"Slide Mantra," marble sculpture exhibited Bienniale in Venice, Italy.
1988	d. Long Island, New York.

"SLIDE MANTRA" MARBLE, BAYFRONT PARK, MIAMI (ALSO EXHIBITED AT THE VENICE BIENNALE, ITALY 1986)

△

BATTER-FRIED SOFT SHELL CRABS WITH ROASTED CORN AND CILANTRO

serves 4

4 large soft shelled crabs, cleaned

1/2 cup rice flour

1/2 cup soda water

1 tablespoon curry powder

2 ears corn, roasted, kernels removed

1/4 cup cilantro

salt and black pepper to taste

chile-infused oil

1 cup balsamic vinegar, reduced to syrup consistency

peanut oil for frying

For batter, mix curry powder with rice flour. Whisk in soda water, season with salt and pepper to taste and reserve. In a heavy-bottomed non-reactive sauce pot heat to 350ºF enough oil to cover the crabs. Place crabs in batter to coat thoroughly. Gently remove and submerge in hot oil. Fresh soft shell crabs will pop when deep fried, so a cover may be necessary. Fry until golden brown, (approx. 2-3 minutes). Remove from oil. Drain on a paper towel. Place crabs on warm plates. Garnish with corn, cilantro, chile oil, and balsamic syrup.

Mondavi Fumé Blanc 1994,
Napa Valley California

"SLIDE MANTRA" MARBLE, BAYFRONT PARK, MIAMI (ALSO EXHIBITED AT THE VENICE BIENNALE, 1986)

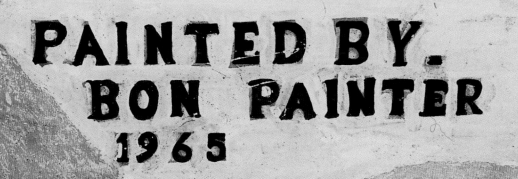

BON PAINTER
ARTIST

"… pull this dam saddle off and set me free."

1917   b. Stillwell, Oklahoma.

1935   Joined Army, trained as a cook.

1950   Became a Mercenary Soldier.

1960   Moved to Watts, OK, became the town drunk, lived in a turned over school bus with a monkey across from the City Post Office. Learned to play the Stradivarius Violin he got during the war.

1962   Began painting as a social critic of local citizens, paintings nailed on trees around his yard.

1965   "The CrosEyed Talking Horse, Painted by Bon Painter - 1965."

1969   Shot his sewing machine. Was frequently arrested (so he could cook for the staff and inmates of the local jail).

1973   Painted "Ask for Nothing in the World Dish."

1974   Painted "Hole Rowlers, Preacher Forked Head."

1975   Painted "One Thing We Know Who Didnet Do It."

1977   Painted "Start from the Grand Old Opera" (Local citizens dancing).

1978   Painted "Look - Dog Population to Dam Many," on a Servel Electrolux Kerosene Refrigerator Door.

1979   Shot his refrigerator.

1980   Painted "As a Tree Falls, So Shall It Lays,"and "Funeral and Burial Service is Now Under Way for the Fort Wayne Unknown Solder."

1981   Painted "My Lands Them Crazy Painters Has Bought This Old Place Back, My Its Wors Than Edna=Even=Bob-Cats . . . I Have A Nice What."

1983   d. Watts, Oklahoma (Buried between towns, Long and Short, Oklahoma).

DETAIL FROM "LOOK - DOG POPULATION TOO DAM MANY" 1978
PREVIOUS TWO PAGES: "THE CROSEYED TALKING HORSE" WITH "WILD THING STEW AND WHITE LIGHTING COOLER"

WILD THING STEW
serves 4-6

Bon Painter loved dining on cooters (river turtles) squirrels, and wood peckers. He prepared the meat as a stew with garden vegetables and herbs that were handy. He usually added a little of whatever he was drinking at the time to the pot!

1-2 pounds meat (cooter, squirrel, woodpecker, beef chuck, chicken or pork), cubed

2-3 tablespoons all-purpose flour

2-3 tablespoons oil (shortening, olive oil, etc)

1/2 teaspoon salt and pepper

4 cups water

2 cups beer, red wine or white wine or 1 cup vodka

10 small onions, peeled or scallions trimmed

6 carrots cleaned but not peeled, cut into chunks

6 medium potatoes, peeled

1/2 cup peas and/or corn

some herbs (basil, rosemary, thyme, parsley, dandilion leaves, garlic and red chiles)

Dust meat with flour and brown on all sides in a large iron skillet. Add booze and bring to a boil. Add water, salt and pepper and all vegetables except herbs. Bring to a boil, cover and simmer for a minimum of 2 hours. Stir gently occasionally. Add herbs and simmer for 30 minutes. Garnish with sprigs of fresh herbs.

WHITE LIGHTNING COOLER
serves 4-6

Equal Parts:

red wine

7-up® or Sprite®

white lightning or vodka

Mix ingredients in a jug and serve in a fruit jar with ice. If you have it. . . you can top with a slice of fruit (peach, pear, apple or strawberry).

HOT CORN PIE
serves 4-6

1 1/2 cups cracker crumbs (loose)

1/2 cup melted butter

1 1/2 cups milk

2 cups fresh or frozen corn

1/2 teaspoon salt

1/2 teaspoon pepper (white if you have it)

2 tablespoons finely chopped onions

2 tablespoons all-purpose flour

2 eggs beaten

1 jalapeño pepper chopped (no seeds)

Combine crumbs and melted butter. With half the mixture, line a 9 inch cast iron skillet or pie pan to form a pie shell. Combine in a sauce pan, 1 cup milk, corn, salt, pepper, jalapeño and onion. Bring to boil and simmer for 3 minutes. Blend flour with remaining milk and stir it slowly into sauce pan mixutre and stir under low heat until thickened. Allow to cool a little, then add the eggs, stirring vigorously. Pour batter into lined skillet and sprinkle with remaining crumbs.

Bake in a preheated oven (400°F) for 15 to 30 minutes or until firm. Cut into wedges and serve.

GOOD PEACH COBBLER
serves 6

1 egg

1 cup sugar

4 tablespoons butter, melted

1/3 cup milk

1/2 cup all-purpose flour

2 teaspoons baking powder

1/4 teaspoon salt

4 cups sliced and peeled fresh or frozen peaches

1/4 teaspoon ground nutmeg

Beat egg, 1/2 cup sugar, butter, and milk. Sift together baking powder, flour and salt. Beat into milk and egg mixture and set aside. Combine sugar and nutmeg and pour into a greased baking pan (10"x10"x2"). Gently pour milk mixture onto the top of the peach mixture and smooth over surface. Bake at 375°F for 30 minutes or until golden on top. Serve warm or cold.

DETAIL FROM "MY LANDS THEM CRAZY PAINTERS HAS BOUGHT THIS OLD PLACE BACK, MY ITS WORS THAN EDNA = EVEN = BOB-CATS... I HAVE A NICE WHAT"

ABOVE: "SWAN SPIRIT" © 1994 MICHAEL PARKES, OIL ON WOOD, 50X65CM, OPPOSITE: "THE JUGGLER" ©1994 MICHAEL PARKES, OIL ON WOOD, 110X90CM (COURTESY: STELTMAN GALLERY AND EDITIONS, AMSTERDAM, THE NETHERLANDS) WITH "GRILLED SALMON ON ASPARAGUS"

> ## "I don't see myself primarily as an artist. I am a student of metaphysics. My art is not to me the end result but rather a means to an end — a means to describe, record and sometimes to help me in my exploration of the universe around me and my relationship to it."

1944	b. in Sikeston, Missouri.
1957	Graduated University of Kansas.
1965	Taught at the University of Ohio.
1970	Traveled with his family to Europe and Asia to study.
1973	Taught graphics in Florida.
1975	Moved to Malaga, Spain.
1977	Began large scale paintings including "Oasis," "St. George," "Mars," "Broken Promises," and "The Juggler's Mistress."
1982	Began stone lithograph series including "Puppetmaster," and "Practice Ring," "Swan King," "Aditi," and "A Gift for the Disillusioned Man."
1991	MICHAEL PARKES: DRAWINGS AND STONE LITHOGRAPHS (Steltman Editions, Amsterdam).
1992	Began Bronze series including "Flight of Fancy" and "Angel of Dawn."
1993	MICHAEL PARKES: 1977-1992 (Steltman Editions, Amsterdam).
1998	Lives with wife Maria in Malaga, Spain.

"ANGEL OF DAWN"

" After many years in Spain, some of the things we'd like to include just would not translate well in the States. I would only know the proportions using Spanish ingredients. For example our tomatoes and green peppers are very different than the ones in the States."

"So we decided on two things that would translate well as the ingredients are more or less the same in taste. They are truly real favorites in our household."

– Maria Parkes

CRÈME FRAÎCHE

2 cups heavy cream

2 tablespoons buttermilk

Mix together and put in a bowl, cover with plastic wrap and let stand overnight in the warmest part of the kitchen. Store in the refrigerator for 4 hours to allow further thickening.

Beringer Chardonnay 1995, Napa Valley, California

GRILLED SALMON
serves 2

2 salmon steaks, 1 inch thick

4 slices large sweet onion

1 lemon, squeezed

1 tablespoon butter

2 sprigs fresh dill

crème fraîche

Prepare your grill fire. Place the two steaks into boiling water with lemon juice and bring to a boil again.

Immediately remove and drain. On a grilling tray, place the salmon on top of large slices of sweet onion.

Cover salmon with the lemon juice. Add a dab of butter and dill.

Grill for about 10 minutes close to the heat. Serve with crème fraîche.

BREAKFAST MUESLI FOR TWO

1/3 cup rolled uncooked oats

1 large Granny Smith apple

1 handful pitted cherries, or other favorite fresh fruit

1 heaping tablespoon ground almonds

3 heaping tablespoons hazlenuts, toasted and coarsely chopped

squeeze of lemon

1-2 tablespoons honey

4 tablespoons cream

Soak oats in water (just covering them) overnight. Do not drain but include the water in the recipe. Next morning peel and grate the apple into the oats. Add the rest of the ingredients and stir. Add more honey if necessary. Enjoy!

ABOVE: "THE LOUVRE" AT MIDNIGHT WITH JOYCE AND A COHIBA, PARIS. BELOW: "THE LOUVRE RAINBOW," PARIS
OPPOSITE: "THE BANK OF CHINA" WITH "ORANGE GLAZED CHICKEN" ON RANGTHONG WARE™ HONG KONG

"Geometry has always been the underpinning of my architecture."

1917	b. Canton, China, father a banker, mother a musician.
1934	Attended Saint John's middle school in Shanghai. Learned English by reading the Bible and Dickens.
1935	Attended University of Pennsylvania School of Architecture, after two weeks transferred to the School of Architecture, MIT, MA.
1940	Received Bachelor of Architecture degree from MIT, Cambridge, MA.
1942	Entered Harvard's Graduate School of Architecture, studied under Walter Gropius.
1943	Joined the "National Defense Research Committee," in Princeton, NJ. and developed ways of destroying German and Japanese structures during World War II.
1946	Received Masters Degree in Architecture from Harvard.
1948	Met real estate tycoon William Zeckendorf and became his director of Webb and Knapps' architectural division.
1950	Designed "Office Building," for Zeckendorf in Atlanta. Henry Cobb joined Pei's architectural division of Webb and Knapp.
1952	For Zeckendorf, designed "Mile High Center," shopping and office complex, Denver, CO.
1954	"Kips Bay," apartment complex, New York (Webb and Knapp).
1955	Founded "I.M. Pei and Associates," a partnership of Pei, Cobb and Easton Leonard.
1956	"Society Hill," housing complex, Philadelphia, PA.
1959	"The Green Earth Sciences Building," MIT, Cambridge, MA.
1961	"University Plaza," apartment towers, NYC; "Luce Memorial Chapel," Taiwan.
1967	"The National Center for Atmospheric Research," Boulder, CO.
1969	"Tandy House," Fort Worth, TX.
1973	"Herbert F. Johnson Museum of Art," Cornell University, Ithaca, NY.
1976	"Oversea - Chinese Banking Corp. Center," Singapore. "Landau Chemical Engineering Building," MIT, Cambridge, MA.
1977	"Dallas Municipal Administration Center, (City Hall)," Dallas, TX.
1979	"The John F. Kennedy Library," Boston; "National Gallery of Art," Washington, DC.
1982	"Fragrant Hill Hotel," Beijing, China; "Warwick Post Oak Hotel," Houston, TX.
1984	"World Trade Center," Miami, FL.
1990	I.M. PEI by Carter Wiseman (Harry N. Abrams, Inc., Publishers, New York). "Bank of China," Hong Kong; "Gateway Towers," Singapore. "Shinji Shumeikai Bell Tower," Shiga, Japan.
1992	"Grand Louvre Phase I & II," Paris.
1993	"Four Seasons Hotel," NYC.
1996	"Rock and Roll Hall of Fame," Cleveland, OH.
1998	Lives in Manhattan and Katonah, New York.

INVERTED PYRAMID, AT THE LOUVRE

▽

ORANGE-GLAZED CORNISH HENS WITH ROASTED NEW POTATOES
serves 4

2 fresh Cornish hens, cut in half

1 1/2 pounds red skinned potatoes, quartered

1 tablespoon fresh chopped garlic

4 large sprigs fresh rosemary

1/2 cup orange marmalade

2 tablespoons herbes de provence

salt and black pepper to taste

corn oil

Place cornish hens in a heavy-bottomed roasting pan. Season with salt, pepper and herbes de provence. Roast in a pre-heated 350ºF oven for about 30 minutes, or to an internal temperature of 160ºF. Meanwhile, toss the red skinned potatoes with garlic, rosemary, and enough corn oil to coat. Season with salt and pepper to taste. Place in a heavy-bottomed roasting pan and roast in the same oven as the hens. Cook potatoes until tender. Once the hens are cooked through, remove from oven and glaze with orange marmalade. Return to oven, and place under the broiler until caramelized. Serve on warm plates with rosemary potatoes and your favorite vegetable.

Fresh squeezed orange juice or Louis M. Martini Folle Blanche 1996, Somoma Valley, California

MORTON H. MEYERSON SYMPHONY CENTER, DALLAS, TEXAS

CESAR PELLI

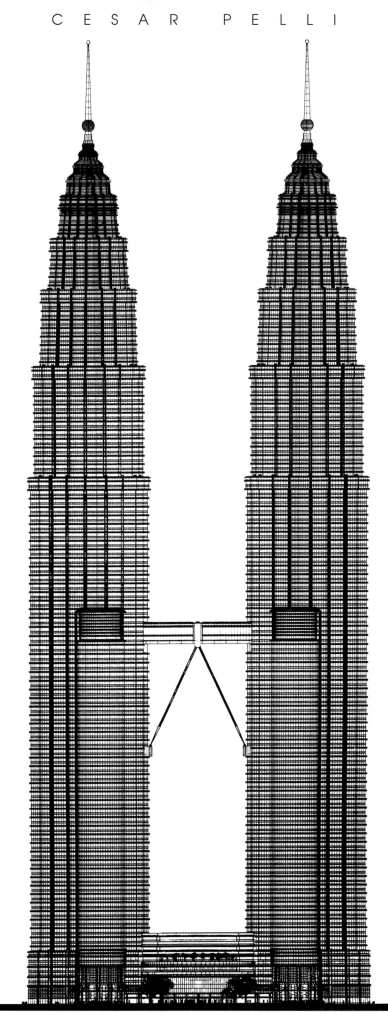

ABOVE: PETRONAS TOWERS, KUALA LUMPUR, MALAYSIA (THE WORLD'S TALLEST BUILDINGS) BELOW: HERRING HALL, RICE UNIVERSITY, HOUSTON, OPPOSITE: "SKETCH OF HERRING HALL" WITH "POLENTA AND TURKEY SAUSAGE" ON ELSA PERETTI'S CRYSTAL STAND, BY TIFFANY & CO.

"Usually great architecture is seen as this thing that mysteriously happens, produced by extraordinary beings. The truth is that it is done by means that everyone has, some more than others..."

1926	b. Tucaman, Argentina.
1950	Received Bachelor of Architecture, University of Tucuman, Argentina.
1954	Received Master of Science Degree in Architecture, Univeristy of Illinois.
1964	Worked for Eero Saarinen and Associates in Hamden, CT.
1965	"Progressive Architecture Award," for "Sunset Mountain Park Complex," Los Angeles, CA.
1968	Worked as director of design for Daniel, Mann, Johnson, and Mendenhall (DMJM), Los Angeles, CA.
1976	Partner for design at Victor Gruen Associates in Los Angeles.
1977	Appointed dean of the Yale Univeristy School of Architecture, New Haven, CT.
1978	"Niagara Falls Winter Garden," Niagara Falls, NY.
1980	Founded architectural firm Cesar Pelli and Associates, New Haven, CT. "The Museum of Modern Art Gallery Expansion and Residential Tower," NYC.
1982	"Four Leaf/Four Oaks Towers," Houston, TX.
1984	"Pacific Design Center," West Hollywood, CA. "Herring Hall," Rice University, Houston, TX. "Rice University Master Plan."
1985	"East Village Student Apartments," University of Hartford, Hartford, CT. "World Financial Center and Winter Garden," New York City, NY.
1986	"181 West Madison Tower," Chicago, IL.
1987	"Canary Wharf Tower, Retail and Assembly Building and Docklands Light Railway Station," London, England; "Yerba Buena Tower," San Francisco, CA.
1988	"Carnegie Hall Tower," New York City, NY; "777 Tower," Los Angeles, CA.
1989	Exhibited "Biennale of Architecture," Buenos Aires, Argentina; "Firm Award," The American Institute of Architects; "Century Tower," New Haven, CT.
1990	CESAR PELLI: BUILDINGS AND PROJECTS 1965-1990 (Rizzoli, New York). "Award of Excellence," American Institute of Steel Construction," "Pacific Design Center," Hollywood, CA.
1992	"North Carolina Blumenthal Performing Arts Center, "Charlotte, NC.
1993	CESAR PELLI: SELECTED AND CURRENT WORKS. (Images Publishing, Australia).
1994	"Frances Lehman Loeb Art Center," Vassar College, Poughkeepsie, NY.
1996	"New North Terminal," Washington National Airport, Washington, D.C.
1997	"Petronas Towers," Kuala, Lumpur, Malaysia.
1998	Lives in New Haven, Connecticut.

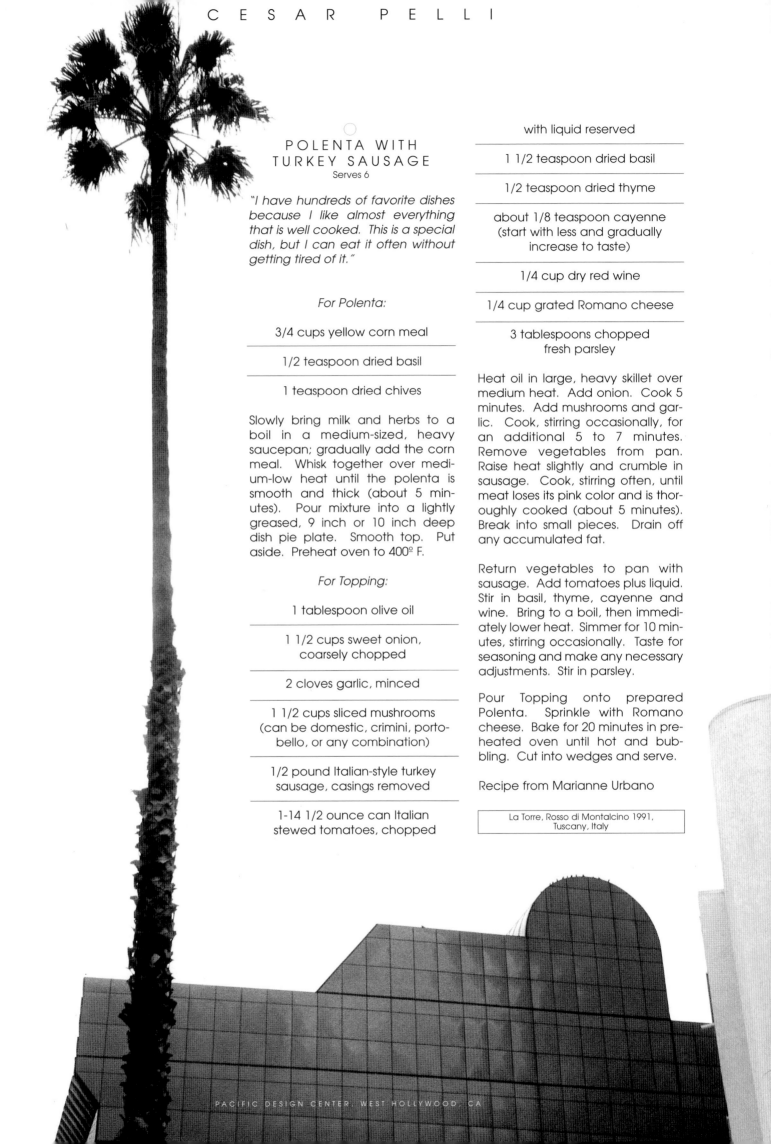

POLENTA WITH TURKEY SAUSAGE
Serves 6

"I have hundreds of favorite dishes because I like almost everything that is well cooked. This is a special dish, but I can eat it often without getting tired of it."

For Polenta:

3/4 cups yellow corn meal

1/2 teaspoon dried basil

1 teaspoon dried chives

Slowly bring milk and herbs to a boil in a medium-sized, heavy saucepan; gradually add the corn meal. Whisk together over medium-low heat until the polenta is smooth and thick (about 5 minutes). Pour mixture into a lightly greased, 9 inch or 10 inch deep dish pie plate. Smooth top. Put aside. Preheat oven to 400° F.

For Topping:

1 tablespoon olive oil

1 1/2 cups sweet onion, coarsely chopped

2 cloves garlic, minced

1 1/2 cups sliced mushrooms (can be domestic, crimini, portobello, or any combination)

1/2 pound Italian-style turkey sausage, casings removed

1-14 1/2 ounce can Italian stewed tomatoes, chopped

with liquid reserved

1 1/2 teaspoon dried basil

1/2 teaspoon dried thyme

about 1/8 teaspoon cayenne (start with less and gradually increase to taste)

1/4 cup dry red wine

1/4 cup grated Romano cheese

3 tablespoons chopped fresh parsley

Heat oil in large, heavy skillet over medium heat. Add onion. Cook 5 minutes. Add mushrooms and garlic. Cook, stirring occasionally, for an additional 5 to 7 minutes. Remove vegetables from pan. Raise heat slightly and crumble in sausage. Cook, stirring often, until meat loses its pink color and is thoroughly cooked (about 5 minutes). Break into small pieces. Drain off any accumulated fat.

Return vegetables to pan with sausage. Add tomatoes plus liquid. Stir in basil, thyme, cayenne and wine. Bring to a boil, then immediately lower heat. Simmer for 10 minutes, stirring occasionally. Taste for seasoning and make any necessary adjustments. Stir in parsley.

Pour Topping onto prepared Polenta. Sprinkle with Romano cheese. Bake for 20 minutes in preheated oven until hot and bubbling. Cut into wedges and serve.

Recipe from Marianne Urbano

La Torre, Rosso di Montalcino 1991, Tuscany, Italy

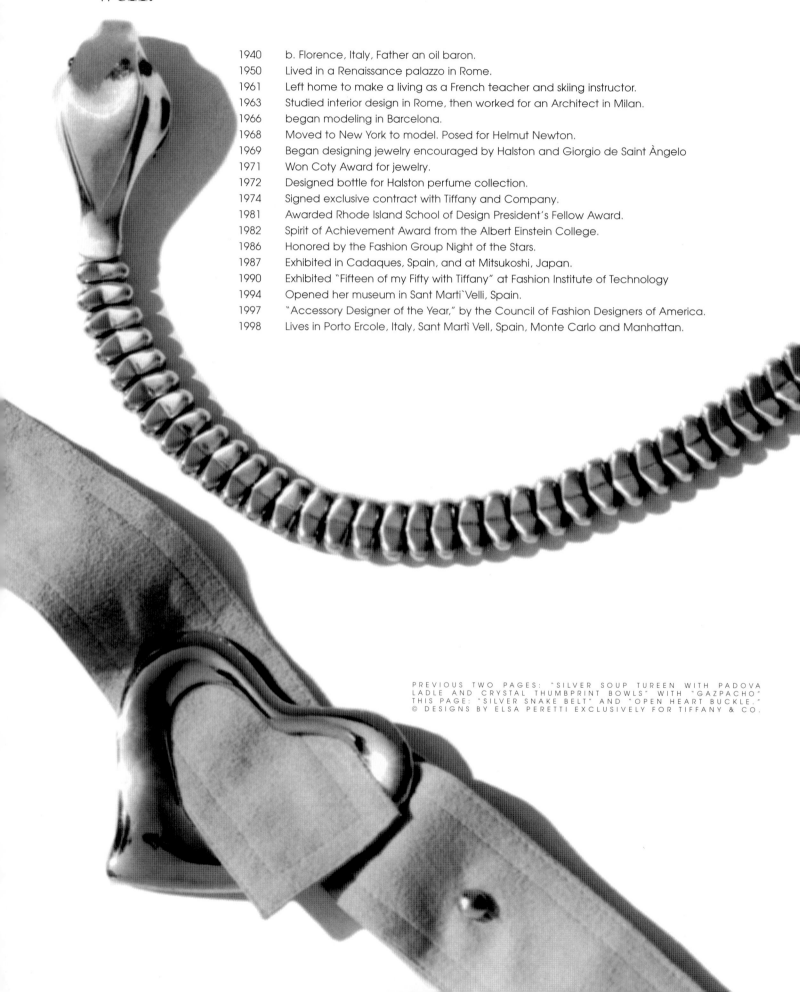

E L S A   P E R E T T I

ARTIST

"Touch is important. I get lots of my inspiration from tactile things, maybe because I don't see very well."

1940	b. Florence, Italy, Father an oil baron.
1950	Lived in a Renaissance palazzo in Rome.
1961	Left home to make a living as a French teacher and skiing instructor.
1963	Studied interior design in Rome, then worked for an Architect in Milan.
1966	began modeling in Barcelona.
1968	Moved to New York to model. Posed for Helmut Newton.
1969	Began designing jewelry encouraged by Halston and Giorgio de Saint Àngelo
1971	Won Coty Award for jewelry.
1972	Designed bottle for Halston perfume collection.
1974	Signed exclusive contract with Tiffany and Company.
1981	Awarded Rhode Island School of Design President's Fellow Award.
1982	Spirit of Achievement Award from the Albert Einstein College.
1986	Honored by the Fashion Group Night of the Stars.
1987	Exhibited in Cadaques, Spain, and at Mitsukoshi, Japan.
1990	Exhibited "Fifteen of my Fifty with Tiffany" at Fashion Institute of Technology
1994	Opened her museum in Sant Marti`Velli, Spain.
1997	"Accessory Designer of the Year," by the Council of Fashion Designers of America.
1998	Lives in Porto Ercole, Italy, Sant Martì Vell, Spain, Monte Carlo and Manhattan.

PREVIOUS TWO PAGES: "SILVER SOUP TUREEN WITH PADOVA LADLE AND CRYSTAL THUMBPRINT BOWLS" WITH "GAZPACHO" THIS PAGE: "SILVER SNAKE BELT" AND "OPEN HEART BUCKLE."
© DESIGNS BY ELSA PERETTI EXCLUSIVELY FOR TIFFANY & CO.

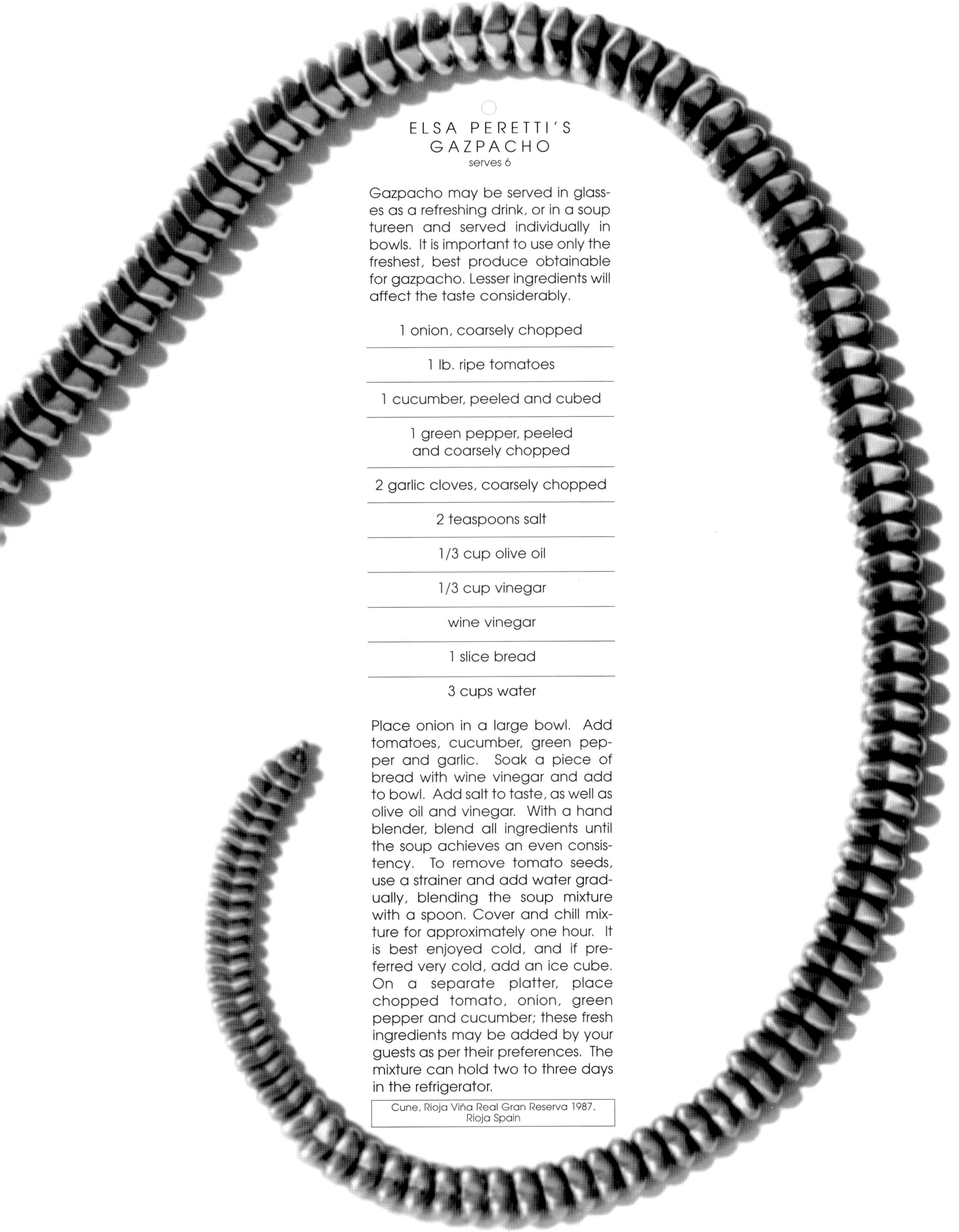

ELSA PERETTI'S
GAZPACHO
serves 6

Gazpacho may be served in glasses as a refreshing drink, or in a soup
tureen and served individually in
bowls. It is important to use only the
freshest, best produce obtainable
for gazpacho. Lesser ingredients will
affect the taste considerably.

1 onion, coarsely chopped

1 lb. ripe tomatoes

1 cucumber, peeled and cubed

1 green pepper, peeled
and coarsely chopped

2 garlic cloves, coarsely chopped

2 teaspoons salt

1/3 cup olive oil

1/3 cup vinegar

wine vinegar

1 slice bread

3 cups water

Place onion in a large bowl. Add
tomatoes, cucumber, green pepper and garlic. Soak a piece of
bread with wine vinegar and add
to bowl. Add salt to taste, as well as
olive oil and vinegar. With a hand
blender, blend all ingredients until
the soup achieves an even consistency. To remove tomato seeds,
use a strainer and add water gradually, blending the soup mixture
with a spoon. Cover and chill mixture for approximately one hour. It
is best enjoyed cold, and if preferred very cold, add an ice cube.
On a separate platter, place
chopped tomato, onion, green
pepper and cucumber; these fresh
ingredients may be added by your
guests as per their preferences. The
mixture can hold two to three days
in the refrigerator.

Cune, Rioja Viña Real Gran Reserva 1987,
Rioja Spain

ABOVE/BELOW: HOTEL SANTA FE, "EURO DISNEY" PARIS

ABOVE/BELOW: "LAS VEGAS LIBRARY" LAS VEGAS, NV

BELOW: "CAPTIVE CACTUS" AT THE HOTEL SANTA FE, PARIS

OPPOSITE: "RED CHILE ENCHILADAS" LAS VEGAS LIBRARY, NV

"I don't think of New Mexico as a region. I think of it as a force that has entered my system, a force that is composed of many things. Here, one is aimed toward the sky and at the same time remains rooted in the earth with geological and cultural past. The lessons to be learned here about responding to the forces of place can be implemented anywhere."

1936	b. Lebanon, Missouri.
1957	Studied at the University of New Mexico, Albuquerque, NM.
1962	Received Bachelor of Architecture from Columbia University, NYC.
1963	Awarded "William Kinne Fellows Memorial Traveling Fellowship," Columbia.
1967	Founded architectural firm "Antoine Predock Architect."
1970	"Predock House and Studio," Albuquerque, NM.
1973	"Kaminsky House" and "The Citadel Apartments," Albuquerque, NM.
1976	"Art Building," Univeristy of New Mexico, and "Mountain House," Albuquerque, NM.
1977	"Chant House," and "Albuquerque Museum," Albuquerque, NM.
1978	"Schwendi Restaurant," Taos Ski Valley, Taos, NM.
1982	"Rio Grande Nature Center," Albuquerque, NM.
1985	Awarded "Rome Prize," (Prix di Roma), The American Academy in Rome.
1986	"Nelson Fine Arts Center," Arizona State University, Tempe, AZ.
1987	"American Heritage Center and Art Museum," University of Wyoming, Laramie, WY; "Las Vegas Central Library and Children's Discovery Museum," Las Vegas, NV; "Rosenthal House," Manhattan Beach, CA; "Fuller House," Scottsdale, AZ.
1989	"Zuber House," Phoenix, AZ.
1991	"Venice House," Los Angeles, CA; "Winandy House," Phoenix, AZ. TERRANCE OF RAIN: AN ITALIAN SKETCH BOOK (Recursos Press, Santa Fe).
1992	"Hotel Santa Fe, Euro-Disney," Marne-la-Vallèe, France. "Institute of American Indian Arts, Museum,"Santa Fe, NM.
1993	"Arizona Museum of Science," Phoenix, AZ. "Ventana Vista Elementary School," Tuscon, AZ; "Center for Integrative Studies Expansion," Stanford University, Palo Alto, CA. "Turtle Creek House," Dallas, TX.
1994	"Social Sciences and Humanities Building," University of California at Davis. ANTOINE PREDOCK: ARCHITECT (Rizzoli International Publications, NY).
1995	"Hispanic Cultural Center," Albuquerque, NM; "Tampa Museum of Science," Tampa, FL.
1996	"School of Music," University of California, Santa Cruz, CA. "Spencer Theatre," Ruidoso, NM.
1997	"Nano Technology Building," Rice Univeristy, Houston, TX.
1998	Lives in Albuquerque, New Mexico.

◇

THE SHED'S
RED CHILE SAUCE
(Santa Fe, NM)
serves 4-6

1 tablespoon shortening

---

1 tablespoon flour

1/3-1/2 cup chile molido
(ground red chile)

---

1 clove garlic

---

3 cups water

---

1 teaspoon salt

Heat 1 tablespoon shortening in 2 quart saucepan. Add 1 tablespoon flour and brown. Blend 1/3 to 1/2 cup chile molido (ground red chile) with 1 clove garlic in 3 cups water. Add 1 teaspoon salt and mix with flour mixture. Stir and simmer for 20 to 30 minutes.

△

RED CHILE
ENCHILADAS
serves 4-6

12 blue corn tortillas

---

10 ounces grated monterey jack
or cheddar cheese

---

4 ounces fresh finely chopped
white onion

---

4 ounces shredded green
leaf lettuce

---

4 ounces chopped ripe tomatoes

To soften tortillas, place in 300ºF oven for 5-7 minutes or in a microwave for 20-30 seconds. Once all the tortillas are softened divide the cheese and onion evenly and place in the middle of each tortilla. (Saving 1/3 of cheese for topping later). Roll each tortilla into a tube shape making sure to have the seam on the bottom. Place the filled tortillas in a lightly buttered, large casserole, side by side, one deep. Top with red chile sauce and place in a 350ºF oven until heated through, about 20-30 minutes. Top with extra cheese, shredded lettuce, and chopped tomatoes. Serve with fresh chiles and tortilla chips.

Dos Equis, Mexico, with Lime

ABOVE: "EMILIO PUCCI DRESS" WITH HIS FAVORITE AUTOMOBILE. OPPOSITE: "SPAGHETTE AL ESTATE"

"Flowers of all colors grow together harmoniously in the fields and almost any colors combined look beautiful together."

1914	b. Naples, Italy, father a Marchese, mother a Contessa.
1933	Graduated from Ginnasio Licio Galilio, Florence.
1934	A member of the Italian Olympic ski team
1935	After two years studying agriculture at the University of Milan he moved to the United States and attended the University of Georgia.
1936	Received a skiing scholarship to Reed college, Portland, OR.
1939	Graduated with a Master of Arts in Social Sciences and designed the Reed college ski team uniform.
1941	Received a Doctorate in Political Science from the University of Florence.
1942	Became a Lieutenant in the Italian Air Force.
1948	Photographed in ski clothes of his own design and was published in Harpers Bazaar; ski outfit designs sold to White Stag and sold through Lord and Taylor.
1949	Opened clothing boutique in Capri, created Capri pants.
1954	Received Neiman-Marcus Fashion Award.
1960	Received Sporting Look Designers Award.
1965	Radical hostess uniforms for Braniff Airways; introduced in Acapulco.
1966	Introduced Balinese wrap skirt after a trip to Bali. Created Vivari, his first perfume.
1967	Designed cotton sheets and towels for Spring Mills.
1971	Designed emblem for the Apollo 15 Space Mission for NASA.
1974	Introduced designs for Rosenthal china of Germany.
1977	Designed limited edition Lincoln Continental. Had boutiques in Florence, New York, Rome, Capri, Paris, Munich, Basel, Tel Aviv, and Atlanta. Designed hostess uniforms for Gulf Air.
1981	Wrote article for the International Herald Tribune, Designed for Princess Diana.
1991	PUCCI: A RENAISSANCE IN FASHION by Shirley Kennedy (Abberville Press, New York, London, Paris)
1992	d. Florence, Italy.

"My prints are ornamental designs worked in continuous motion; however they are placed there is rhythm."

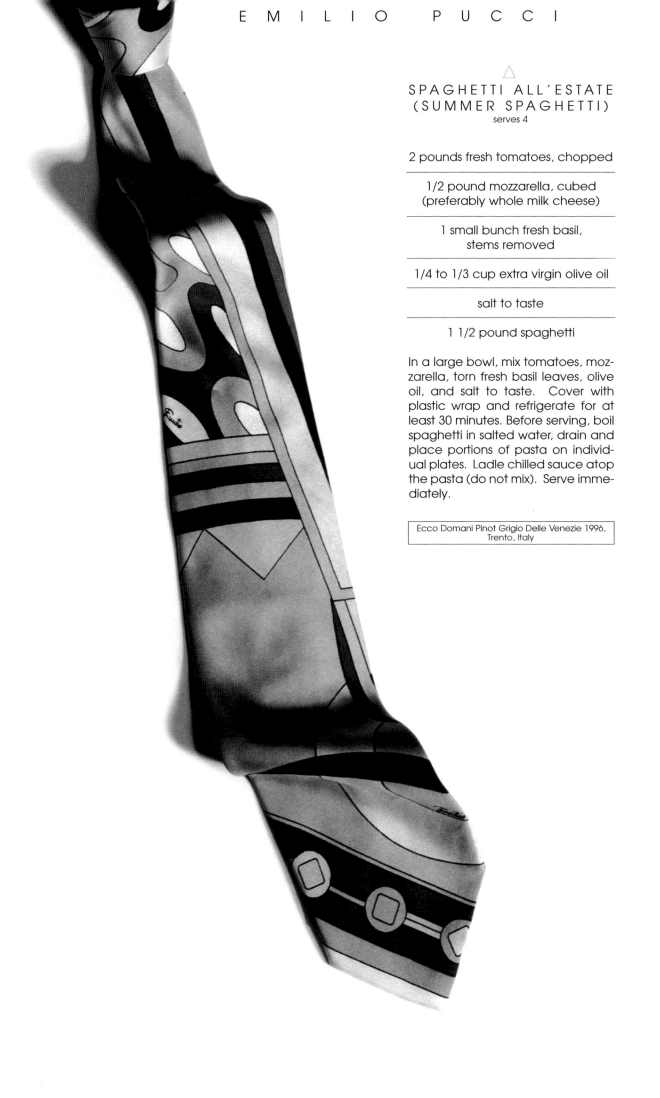

SPAGHETTI ALL'ESTATE (SUMMER SPAGHETTI)

serves 4

2 pounds fresh tomatoes, chopped

1/2 pound mozzarella, cubed
(preferably whole milk cheese)

1 small bunch fresh basil,
stems removed

1/4 to 1/3 cup extra virgin olive oil

salt to taste

1 1/2 pound spaghetti

In a large bowl, mix tomatoes, mozzarella, torn fresh basil leaves, olive oil, and salt to taste. Cover with plastic wrap and refrigerate for at least 30 minutes. Before serving, boil spaghetti in salted water, drain and place portions of pasta on individual plates. Ladle chilled sauce atop the pasta (do not mix). Serve immediately.

Ecco Domani Pinot Grigio Delle Venezie 1996,
Trento, Italy

ABOVE: "GRANITA RESTAURANT" MALIBU, CALIFORNIA   OPPOSITE: "LOBSTER SALAD, SQUAB WITH NOODLE CAKE, AND BERRY COBBLER"

"And as Picasso's style became less complicated later in life, so has cuisine in America left behind the showing - off typical of youth, maturing to a greater simplicity." – PUCK

1949	b. Wolfgang Puck, St. Veit, Austria, mother a hotel chef.
1964	Apprenticed at L'Oustean de Baumaniere in Provencie, France.
1968	Apprenticed at Hotel de Paris, Monaco.
1970	Apprenticed at Maxim's, Paris, France.
1973	Moved to the United States, worked at Indianapolis' La Tour.
1976	Became chef and part-owner of Ma Maison, Los Angeles.
1981	MODERN FRENCH COOKING, by Wolfgang Puck (Random House, Inc. NYC).
1982	Married Barbara Lazaroff (Dress design by Zandra Rhodes).
1982-98	Continued below.

"As a designer, I take a multitude of elements, and from chaos try to create a functioning system that incorporates beauty, harmony, excitement, and a sense of joy and well-being." – LAZAROFF

1953	b. Barbara Lazaroff, Bronx, New York.
1971	Studied bio chemistry and experimental psychology along with theater arts, set design, and lighting.
1979	Began her career as an architectural and interior designer.
1982	With husband Wolfgang Puck created "Spago," West Hollywood, CA.
1983	Created "Chinois on Main," LA; Founded "Imaginings Interior Design," (Lazaroff).
1984	Created "Eureka Brewery and Restaurant."
1986	THE WOLFGANG PUCK COOKBOOK, by Wolfgang Puck (Random House, Inc. NY).
1988	Founded "Wolfgang Puck Food Company."
1989	Created "Postrio Restaurant," San Francisco, CA.
1990	Created "Eureka Brewery and Restaurant," Los Angeles, CA; Created "Spago Tokyo."
1991	WOLFGANG PUCK: ADVENTURES IN THE KITCHEN by Wolfgang Puck (Random House, NY).
1992	Created "Granita," Mailbu, CA; Lazarott "Platinum Circle Award," Hotel and Restaurant Design International Magazine.
1993	Created "Wolfgang Puck Cafè," at Universal City Walk, Los Angeles, CA. (Also in MGM Grand, Las Vegas, NV., Santa Monica, CA., San Francisco, and Cairo.)
1994	Awarded "Humanitarian of the Year," also "Spago, Restaurant of the Year," by The James Beard Foundation.
1996	Created "Spago," Chicago, IL.
1998	Live in Los Angeles with their sons Cameron and Byron.

• •

○
FRANK'S LOBSTER SALAD
serves 8

Spago House Salad Dressing
(recipe follows)

1/2 lb. cooked fresh lobster meat, tails or claws, cut into thin slices

4 cups packed Chino Chopped Vegetable Salad (recipe follows)

2 cups assorted greens (curly endive, baby lettuces, chicory, etc.)

fresh caviar, optional

Lightly brush eight 3/4-cup ramekins with Spago salad dressing. For each portion, arrange a few pieces (about 1 ounce) of lobster on the bottom. Fill with 1/2 cup chopped salad and pat down well to fill the cup and level the top. For presentation, toss the greens with just enough dressing to coat the leaves. Divide equally and arrange in the center of each of 8 salad plates. Invert a cup of salad onto the greens and rap gently as necessary to unmold. Spoon a little caviar on top, if desired. Serve immediately.

SPAGO HOUSE SALAD DRESSING

2 large shallots, minced

1 tablespoon Dijon mustard

2 tablespoons zinfandel or other red wine vinegar

2 tablespoons sherry wine vinegar

1/2 cup extra virgin olive oil

1/2 cup vegetable oil

salt & freshly ground white pepper

In a small bowl, whisk together the shallots and the mustard. Whisk in the vinegars, then the olive and vegetable oil. Season with salt and pepper to taste. Transfer to a covered container and refrigerate until needed.

CHINO CHOPPED VEGETABLE SALAD

For the Mustard Vinaigrette:

1 tablespoon Dijon Mustard

3 tablespoons sherry wine vinegar

1/2 cup extra-virgin olive oil

1/2 cup almond or safflower oil

salt

freshly ground white pepper

For the Salad:

1 tablespoon olive oil

1/2 cup diced fresh artichoke bottoms

salt

freshly ground white pepper

1/2 cup carrots, diced

1/2 cup green beans, diced

1/2 cup red onion, diced

1/2 cup radicchio, diced

1/2 cup fresh corn kernels

1/2 cup celery, diced

1/2 cup ripe avocado, diced

1/4 cup tomato, peeled, seeded and chopped

4 teaspoons Parmesan cheese, grated

First prepare the vinaigrette by combining the mustard and vinegar in a small bowl. Slowly whisk in the oils. Season to taste with salt and pepper and set aside. Whisk again when ready to serve.

In a small skillet, heat the olive oil. Season the diced artichokes lightly with salt and pepper and sauté until al dente, about 3 minutes. Transfer to a large bowl and let cool.

Blanch the carrots and beans by placing each into a fine mesh basket. Set the basket into a pot of boiling salted water and cook until al dente, 2 to 3 minutes.

Plunge into cold water to stop the cooking process. Drain, cool, and add to the artichokes. Add the onion, radicchio, corn, and celery. When ready to serve, dice the avocado and the tomato and add to the other vegetables. Reserving a little vinaigrette, toss the vegetables with the vinaigrette, sprinkle with the grated cheese, and toss again. Correct seasoning to taste.

CHINOIS ROASTED SQUAB ON PAN-FRIED NOODLES WITH SPICY MUSHROOM SAUCE
serves 2 to 4

4 ounces Chile Pasta Dough (recipe follows)

2 tablespoons peanut oil

2 tablespoons sesame oil

For the Spicy Mushroom Sauce:

1 tablespoon peanut oil

1 cup shiitake and oyster mushrooms, cut into julienne

1/2 cup dry red wine

1/4 cup plum wine

1/2 cup brown chicken or veal stock

1 tablespoon unsalted butter

freshly ground pepper

1 large garlic clove, minced

1 green onion, minced

1/4 fresh ginger, minced

1/8 teaspoon chile pepper flakes, chopped very fine

1 one-pound squab

salt and freshly ground pepper

1 tablespoon peanut oil

1 bunch watercress

1/2 tablespoon rice wine vinegar

1 teaspoon sesame oil

salt and freshly ground pepper

To prepare the pan-fried noodles, roll out the dough as thin as possible and, using a sharp knife or a pasta machine, cut into 1/4-inch noodles. Bring a medium pot of water to a boil. Add a pinch of salt and a little olive oil and cook the pasta al dente.

Rinse under cold water, drain well, and dry thoroughly. In an 8-inch nonstick skillet, over moderate heat, heat 2 tablespoons each of peanut and sesame oils. Spread the noodles evenly over the pan and fry until crisp and golden brown.

Turn and brown the other side. The pancake should be crispy on the outside and still slightly soft on the inside. Reserve. (This can be prepared early in the day and reheated at serving time in 1 tablespoon each peanut oil and butter.)

Preheat the grill/oven to 400º F.

Domaine Drouhin Pinot Noir 1995, Yamhill County, Oregon

Recipe continued on page 228.

ABOVE: "NAAM PRIK DIP" WITH RANTHONG STAINLESS WARE   BELOW: "THAI HOME INDUSTRIES BUILDING"
OPPOSITE: "BEEF AND BITTER GOURD" WITH "SILVER HEADRESS" FROM AKHA REGION, THAILAND

150

"I kept looking at my father's knives all the time and found that each was crafted from one piece of steel.. he was my inspiration."

1925	b. Petchury, Thailand.
1959	Established "Thai Home Industries," Bangkok.
1972	Began designing and producing tableware under label "Rangthong."™
1975	Designed "Thai Home Industries Building," Bangkok.
1986	"Stainless Steel Cutlery," Collection of the Museum of Modern Art, NYC.
1993	d. Bangkok, Thailand.

NAAM PRIK DIP

This dish is a traditional Thai country food. Each part of Thailand has its own type of Naam Prik (North, Central, South).

This was Jaivid Rangthong's favorite dish. Daily meals would not be complete without Naam Prik. Jaivid's wife, Reena, would prepare all the ingredients, and Jaivid would make the Naam Prik himself.

4 large cloves garlic, peeled

1 teaspoon roasted shrimp paste*

2 pieces dried shrimp, pounded (about 1 teaspoon)

1/2 teaspoon palm sugar, or light brown sugar

1/4 teaspoon fish sauce

2 limes

4 tiny red Thai chiles (or 2 small green chiles - not as hot)

Fresh vegetables for dipping (e.g. fresh cucumber, green beans, round egg plants)

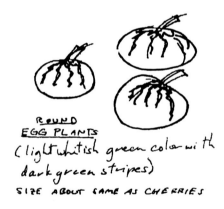

ROUND EGG PLANTS
(light whitish green color with dark green stripes)
SIZE ABOUT SAME AS CHERRIES

Put 2 cloves of garlic and 2 tiny Thai chiles (or 1 green chile) in a mortar and crush slightly. Add to the mor-tar 1 teaspoon roasted shrimp paste, remaining chiles, and 2 more cloves garlic. Grind to even consis-tency. Add 1/2 teaspoon palm sugar and mix well. Add dried shrimp and fish sauce and mix well.

Squeeze in juice from both limes and mix. The Naam Prik should have a slightly watery consistency - almost like a paste but with more liquid.

For tasting, dip a fresh green bean in the Naam Prik. The taste should be salty, sour, and slightly sweet. Add more fish sauce, palm sugar, or lime juice if necessary to the individ-ual's taste.

Serve in a small dip bowl. Garnish with one red chile.

In Thailand, we would also serve fried fish with this dip, such as "Plaa Too," a white fish similar to the trout or sardine. There, the fish would be steamed, then fried. May we sug-gest a substitute of broiled trout or broiled sardine slightly salted.

*Note: To roast shrimp paste, pre-heat burner to medium heat and add paste (found at Asian markets) to a small pan and cook until it starts to smell, about 2-3 min-utes. Do not burn! Flip to the other side and cook as well.

STIR FRY BEEF AND BITTER GOURD VEGETABLE

2 small servings

Jaivid's wife Reena prepared this dish for him twice a week.

6-7 ounces beef, filet or rib eye cut

1 bitter gourd, 6 inches long (available in Asian markets - looks like a shriveled green cucumber with a slight bitter taste)

1 teaspoon black bean paste

1/2 teaspoon salt

1 teaspoon dark, thick soy sauce

3/4 teaspoon corn starch

1 1/2 tablespoons vegetable oil

1 clove garlic, peeled and crushed

2 cups steamed jasmine rice

Cut the bitter gourd in half length-wise, then thinly slice the halves. Sprinkle the salt over the slices and toss in a bowl. Let stand for about 2 minutes. Use 2 cups of water to rinse the slices. Drain and pat dry. Set aside. Mix 1/2 teaspoon corn-starch with 1/2 cup water in a small cup. Set aside.

Slice the beef very thinly and cut into small strips. Mix together 1/4 teaspoon corn starch, soy sauce, 1/2 tablespoon oil, 1/2 teaspoon black bean paste. Add beef and marinate for 1 hour. Heat wok to medium high heat. Add 1 table-spoon oil. When the oil is hot, add 1 clove crushed garlic and 1/2 tea-spoon black bean paste. Quick stir fry for about 15 seconds. Add to the wok the marinated beef, followed by the sliced bitter gourd. Stir fry until beef is medium rare, about 2-3 minutes. Push the beef and bitter gourd to one side of the wok. Into the center of the wok, pour the mix-ture of water and corn starch. Bring to a boil and stir in the beef with bit-ter gourd and mix well until beef is cooked. If the water mixture has evaporated, add 1/4 cup water and quickly stir fry. Remove from wok and spoon over a plate of steamed Thai jasmine rice.

Singha Lager Beer, Thailand or Mekong with Club Soda and Lemon Wedge

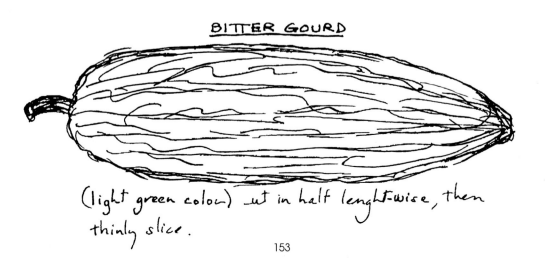

BITTER GOURD

(light green color) cut in half lenghtwise, then thinly slice.

"I knew the wild riders and the vacant land were about to vanish."

1861	b. Canton, New York, father ran a newspaper.
1877	Attended Highland Military Academy, Worchester, MIT, and Vermont Episcopal Institute of Burlington, VT.
1879	Studied at the School of Fine Arts, Yale University, New Haven, CT.
1880	After father's death, he traveled to Kansas City, then to Arizona and New Mexico, to paint and sketch the "Wild West." Rode with Cavalry.
1885	Began selling drawings for illustrations in Harpers Weekly, Outing, and St. Nicholas magazines.
1887	Began illustrations for Theodore Roosevelt's novel, RANCH LIFE AND THE HUNTING TRAIL." Exhibited at the National Academy of Design.
1889	Moved to New Rochelle, NY. Painted "A Dash for the Timber."
1890	Illustrated Longfellow's SONG OF HIAWATHA. Traveled to Montana and sketched the cavalry; Painted "Aiding a Comrade," painting.
1895	Painted "The Fall of the Cowboy;" Sculpted, First bronze for Tiffany & Co. "The Bronco Buster."
1897	Signed exclusive contract with Collier's to paint six paintings a year.
1898	"The Wicked Pony," and "The Scalp," bronzes. Wrote SUN-DOWN LEFLARE.
1901	"The Cheyenne," bronze; "Fight for the Water Hole," painting.
1902	"Coming Through the Rye," bronze. Wrote JOHN ERMINE OF THE YELLOWSTONE.
1903	"The Mountain Man," bronze; "His First Lesson," painting.
1904	"Polo," bronze.
1905	"The Rattlesnake," bronze. "Coming to the Call," and "Evening on a Canadian Lake," paintings.
1906	"The Outlaw," bronze. Wrote THE WAY OF AN INDIAN. "Radisson and Groseilliers," painting.
1907	"The Buffalo Horse," and "The Horse Thief," bronzes; "Fired On," "Downing the Nigh Leader," and "Early Autumn," paintings.
1908	"Chippewa Bay," "Apache Scouts Listening," " Night Halt of the Calvary," "Shoshone," "Indians Simulating Buffalo," and "The Snow Trail," paintings. "Fired On," purchased by the National Gallery in Washington, DC.
1909	"Trooper of the Plains," and "The Stampede," bronzes; "The Outlier," "The Gossips," "Wolf in the Moonlight," and "Pontiac Club, Canada," paintings.
1909	d. Ridgefield, Connecticut.

☐

GRILLED COWBOY CUT RIBEYE WITH CORN, BISCUITS AND CREAM GRAVY
serves 4

For the Ribeye:

4-22 ounce bone-in ribeyes

---

4 ears corn

---

salt and pepper to taste

---

butter

Season the ribeyes with salt and pepper to taste and grill to desired doneness over a hot charcoal or wood-burning grill. Brush ears of corn with butter, season with salt and pepper to taste and grill until caramelized and tender. Serve with biscuits and cream gravy.

The Macallan 12 year old Scotch

☐

CREAM GRAVY
serves 2

1/4 cup bacon drippings

1/4 cup all purpose flour

3-4 cups milk

---

salt and pepper to taste

Over medium heat, melt drippings in a heavy skillet. Add flour and cook until golden and bubbly. Slowly add milk, whisking until thickening begins. Continue to whisk, adding more milk for a thinner gravy. Salt and pepper to taste. Serve over warm, split biscuits.

☐

BISCUITS
15-20 biscuits

1 pound butter, chilled and cubed

---

4 cups all-purpose flour

---

2 teaspoons baking powder

---

1 teaspoon bakig soda

---

buttermilk

---

salt and pepper to taste

Mix all dry ingredients well, and cut in butter until mixture resembles a coarse cornmeal. Do not overmix. Lightly knead by pressing it out onto a floured surface and folding it in half. Rotate the dough 90ºF between folds. Repeat this procedure five to ten times. The dough should be soft and slightly elastic, but not sticky. Roll out to desired thickness and cut out. Place on a greased or paper-lined baking sheet. Brush the tops with egg wash or milk to aid browning. Bake in preheated 425ºF oven 15-20 minutes. Serve warm.

ABOVE: "ZANDRA RHODES 'ADITI' PORTRAIT" THE ARTIST AS ART PHOTO BY ROBYN BEECHE
OPPOSITE: "SUMMER PUDDING" WITH JOYCE'S MOTHER OF THE BRIDE DRESS DESIGN

"What we find ugly today will be beautiful tomorrow. I'm tired of good taste. I want to do everything wrong and get a result that is of value and valid as well."

1940	b. Chatham, Kent, England, father a lorry driver, mother a senior lecturer in the Fashion Department at Medway College of Art.
1961	Studied fashion design at Medway College of Art, Kent, England.
1964	Studied at the Royal College of Art, School of Textile Design. Met Florentine aristocrat designer Emilio Pucci.
1966	Richard Avedon photographed a Zandra Rhodes scarf for cover of Vogue.
1968	Richard Holley introduced her designs to USA - met Diana Vreeland, NY. Her design's appear in "Women's Wear Daily," and "English Vogue."
1971	Traveled to Australia and Japan - Introduced her work in Tokyo.
1972	"Designs of the Year," English Fashion Trade, had first show in New York City.
1974	"Royal Designer for Industry (RDI)," designed "Princess Anne's Bridal Dress."
1975	Began "Posters," with Barry Lategan. Designed jacket for Princess Margaret.
1977	Introduced "Punk, Conceptual Chic Collection," London.
1978	Solo Exhibition, "Zandra Rhodes,Oriel, Wales, UK," and began "Heads," series.
1979	"Emmy Award," for best costume for CBS, "Romeo and Juliet on Ice." "Best Costume Award," British Association of Film and Television.
1982	Solo Exhibition, "Zandra Rhodes, " La Jolla Museum of Contemporary Art, LaJolla, CA.
1983	Awarded "Britain's Designer," Clothing Export Council and National Eco. Dev. Committee.
1984	THE ART OF ZANDRA RHODES, by Zandra Rhodes (Jonathan Cape Limited, London),
1985	"This is your Life," TV tribute the the Art and Works of Zandra Rhodes (Thames TV). Key Speaker "Aspen Arts Festival," Aspen, CO.
1986	Doctorate, International Fine Arts College, Honoris Causa, (DFA), Miami, FL.
1987	"Doctor of Design," (DD) Honoris Causa, Council for Nat. Academic Awards, UK.
1990	Voted "Number One Textile Designer," in UK by Observer Magazine.
1991	Solo Exhibition "Zandra," Dynasen Gallery, and "Best Show of the Year," Saks Fifth Avenue, New Orleans, LA.
1992	"Fellow of Kent Institute of Art and Design," UK.
1993	Designed table setting for House and Gardens, "Art of Entertaining."
1994	Designed Joyce's dress for Miles and Courtney's Wedding, Miami, FL.
1998	Lives in London.

ZANDRA'S CLASSIC FINE SPINACH SOUP
serves 6

2 large bunches fresh spinach

1 large onion, coarsely chopped

1 potato, cleaned, not peeled and chopped

1 teaspoon fennel seeds

1/2 inch piece fresh ginger root, finely chopped

1 heaping tablespoon cumin

salt and freshly ground pepper

2 chicken stock cubes

sesame seed salt (recipe follows)

red and yellow nasturtium flowers

In a large pan, fill with water about 3 inches along with chicken stock cubes and dissolve. Wash spinach well. Tear leaves away from the larger stems (the smaller stems are fine to leave on). In the large pan with hot stock, push in all spinach leaves, onion, fennel seeds, salt, ginger root, cumin and chopped potato. Bring to a boil. Boil for about 10 minutes. There should be enough liquid to then cover the rapidly softened and collapsed spinach leaves. If not, add more water (about 2 cups). Cool slightly.

Blend (preferably in a food blender). This should then make a soup of a fine creamy consistency, and of a wonderful deep intense green color. Add freshly ground black pepper and check the taste.

It may possibly need more salt and cumin. If needed add more water and another chicken cube (pre-dissolved). Serve hot with floating yellow and red nasturtium flowers and a trail of burnt sesame seed salt.

LOBSTER TAILS WITH SWEETCORN AND WILD RICE

1 lobster tail per person

fresh ginger root

onion

olive oil

salt

lemon

PREVIOUS TWO PAGES: "SPINACH SOUP, SESAME SEED SALT, LOBSTER TAILS WITH SWEET CORN AND WILD RICE, AND FLORAL SALAD

162

sesame seed salt, recipe follows

prepared wild rice

cooked fresh corn on the cob

Boil lobster tails in water to which you have added chopped ginger, onion, salt and a dash of olive oil. Bring to a boil and reduce heat. Simmer for 30 minutes. Serve with slices of lemon and burnt sesame seeds. Tastes delicious served with wild rice and sweetcorn.

Perrier-Jouët Fleur de Champagne 1988, Reims, France

SESAME SEED SALT

Place a tablespoon of sesame seeds in a frying pan and heat until they turn black and jump. Stir so they burn evenly. Put into a pestle and mortar with salt and grind. This is fabulous placed on the table in small salt cellars or bowls and sprinkled on food exactly as salt and pepper are used.

SUMMER PUDDING

This is ideal to make in mid-summer when there is the luxury of masses of summer fruits. Also, it is one dessert that freezes perfectly. It always tastes wonderful and its consistency is totally unaffected by being frozen! I make these puddings six at a time when fruit is at its cheapest and grab all the black and red currants as soon as I see them.

1 loaf sliced white bread

granulated sugar

choice of fruits in season - you can use any combination but currants are essential:

blackcurrants;

redcurrants;

blackberries;

raspberries;

strawberries;

blueberries;

cherries
(halved with pits removed);

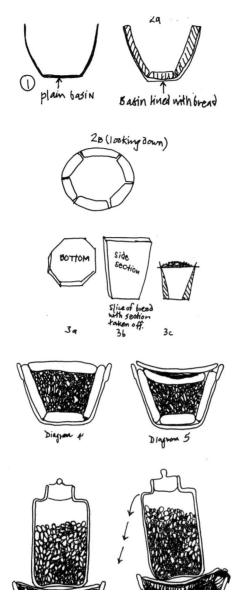

gooseberries;*

rhubarb.*

Fresh cream

*Note: If using gooseberries or rhubarb as additional filler, par-boil in water with extra sugar until softened before adding to rest of fruit.

With a sharp serrated knife, cut off the crusts from the bread. Take a pudding basin, (a china or plastic deep bowl - diagram 1) and completely line with bread leaving no gaps - diagram 2. You probably need to trim the bread slices like this - diagram 3.

Put all fruit in a large saucepan filled with 1/2 inch water and bring just to the boil, then turn off the heat. Add sugar to your personal taste, and stir gently until dissolved but the fruit is still whole and not a pulpy mess. Using a slotted spoon, spoon fruit mixture into bread-lined basin(s) to within 1 inch of the top. Save excess juice and store in refrigerator. Using more sliced bread, make a bread "lid" and put on top - diagram 4.

Find a saucer just a fraction smaller than the top of the basin. Place on top of the bread lid correct way up - diagram 5.

Stand whatever you have that is heavy onto the saucer for 8 hours (e.g. old flat iron, large storage jar filled with beans, etc. - diagram 6).

The reason for the weights is so the fruit juices get pushed into the bread and the two become inseparable. This definitely takes 8 hours.

Important - During the first half hour the weights can change position and sometimes fall over - diagram 7 - so try to arrange so that the containers can lean safely onto a wall, etc., so things don't fall over.

Check periodically. It is best to make these a day in advance, then leave under weights all night, then in the morning remove weights and saucers, cover and put either into the refrigerator for immediate eating, or into the freezer. Before serving, run a knife gently around the edge then turn upside down onto a plate. Pour reserved fruit juice on top until soaked. Serve with a jug of English double cream. Divine!

Recipes continued on page 227.

"ZANDRA RHODES" BY ROBYN BEECHE

"Architecture has developed from the need to order the world in space and time, and like all creative activities, is an expression of an epoch given form by the history of that epoch."

1933	b. Florence, Italy of British parents.
1958	Educated at the Architectual Association in London.
1962	Post Graduate studies at Yale Univeristy, School of Architecute, New Haven, CT.
1963	Founded "Team 4" with wife Su and Wendy and Norman Foster.
1971	Formed architectural firm Piano & Rogers. Won competition, "Centre National d'Art et de Culture Georges - Pompidou," Paris.
1973	Offices and factory for "B&B Italia," Como, Italy.
1974	Factory for "Universal Oil Products," Tadworth, Surrey, England.
1975	Laboratory for "PA Technology," Melborne, Hertfordshire, England. Royal Institute of British Architects Award.
1977	Formed Architectural firm Richard Rogers + Partners, London, England.
1978	Won competition for "Lloyds of London," Headquarters, London, England.
1982	"INMOS Microprocessor Factory," Newport, South Wales. "PA Technology Laboratroies and Corporate Facility," Princeton, NJ.
1984	"Thames Wharf Complex," including studios, housing, and his restaurant, "The River Cafe;" "Industrial Units at Maidenhead," Berkshire, England.
1985	Factory for "Linn Products," Glasgow, Scotland. Awarded the "Royal Gold Medal for Architecture."
1986	Exhibition "New Architecture: Foster, Rogers, Stirling," Royal Academy of Arts, London.
1987	Redevelopment of "Billingsgate Market," London. Won "Civic Trust Award," and "Financial Times Architecture at Work," award. Designed his "Royal Avenue Residence," in London.
1988	"Pump House," Royal Victorial Docks, London. "GRC Headquarters," Lyon, France. RICHARD ROGERS; 1978-1988 (A+U Publishing, Tokyo).
1996	"Hall of Human Rights," Strasbourg.
1998	Lives with wife Ruth in London.

CENTRE CULTUREL D'ART GEORGES POMPIDOU WITH NIKKI DE SAINT-PHALLE AND TINGUELY FOUNTAIN, PARIS
PREVIOUS TWO PAGES: FIRST: "LLOYDS OF LONDON" ENGLAND,   SECOND: "GRILLED SALMON WITH THREE SAUCES"

△

ATLANTIC SALMON WITH GRILLED CORN SAUCE
serves 8

For the Salmon:

1 side fresh Atlantic salmon, pin bones removed

2 tablespoons fresh chopped parsley leaves

2 tablespoons fresh chopped chives

2 tablespoons fresh chopped thyme leaves

olive oil

salt and pepper to taste

Coat the salmon with olive oil and season with salt and pepper. Grill both sides over a hot charcoal or wood-burning grill to desired doneness. Once fish is done, remove and sprinkle with fresh chopped herbs.

Served with grilled corn sauce.

For the Grilled Corn Sauce:

8 ears of corn, peeled

1 medium onion, small diced

2 tablespoons peeled ginger, diced

1 bunch cilantro, chopped

1 quart milk

salt and pepper to taste

Grill the corn cobs until caramelized and tender. Remove the corn from the cobs and reserve both.

In a heavy-bottomed non-reactive sauce pot, sweat the onion and ginger until translucent.

Add the remaining ingredients, including the cobs, and simmer for 20-30 minutes. Remove from heat and let steep for 1 hour. Remove the cobs and transfer to a blender and puree. Pass through a sieve. Adjust seasoning. Served with grilled salmon.

Castello Banfi San Angelo Pinot Grigo 1996, Tuscany, Italy

△

ROGERS' ROCKET SALAD
serves 8

2 pounds fresh rocket (arugula), washed and dried

1/2 cup extra virgin olive oil

1/2 cup fresh squeezed lemon juice

salt and pepper to taste

parmiggiano reggiano cheese

fresh sliced lemon

Whisk the olive and lemon juice together. Season to taste. Dress the greens and toss. Serve with fresh lemon slices and shaved parmiggiano reggiano cheese.

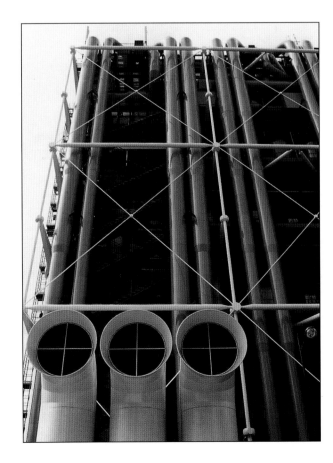

ABOVE: "ARGENTINE FLANK STEAK" WITH "SKETCH FOR FOREST RANGER," 1967, 24"X19"X19" SILKSCREEN ON ACETATE AND
PHILIPPE STARCK'S STEAK KNIFE FOR LAGUIOLE OPPOSITE: "UNTITLED," 1989, 5'X5', OIL ON CANVAS, WITH "STONE CRAB CLAW PASTA"

"It's scary, putting a new vision together that can change your thinking or someone else's. I think it can be done. You can make something so beautiful, or so serious, or so ugly that it scrambles your mind and changes your attitude toward seeing things."

1933	b. Grand Forks, North Dakota, to mother of Norwegian descent and father of Swedish descent.
1948	Won art scholarship from Minneaspolis Art Institute (age 14).
1953	Studied Art at University of Minnesota.
1954	Painted billboards for General Outdoor Advertising (Coca-Cola,® Davy Crockett, Corby's Whiskey).
1955	Received scholarship, Art Students League, NYC.
1958	Worked for Artkraft Strauss painting billboards in Times Square and Brooklyn NY.
1959	Attended drawing classes with Claes Oldenberg, Henry Parsons, Jack Youngerman and Robert Indiana.
1962	First one-man show; Green Gallery, NYC. Also in Sidney Jamis Gallery, NYC.
1963	Received mural commission for New York World's Fair. Exhibited work at Museum of Modern Art and Guggenheim Museum, NYC, and The Chicago Art Insititue.
1966	Exhibited F-I II at Moderna Museet, Stockholm, Sweden.
1969	Exhibited Horse Blinders at Leo Castelli Gallery, NYC.
1972	Arrested in Washington, D.C., as a Vietnam war protester with Dr. Benjamin Spock.
1980	Exhibited at the Palazzo Grazzi in Venice "Pop Art: Evolution of a Generation," with Jim Dine, Roy Lichtenstein, Claes Oldenberg, George Sagan and Tom Wesselman.
1981	"Star Theif," selected by Miami International Airport. Controversy prevents installation.
1984	Recommended by Philip Jonhson for mural commission at the Four Seasons Restaurant in Manhattan; "Flowers, Fish and Females."
1985	"Ladies of the Opera Terrace," for the Opera Terrace, Stockholm, Sweden.
1989	Scarf painting for Louis Vuitton, Paris.
1990	"Welcome to the Water Planet," Museum of Modern Art, NYC.
1991	Exhibited in Central Hall of Artists, Tretyakon Museum, Moscow.
1996	"The Italian Riviera Cups ," for Illy, Trieste, Italy.
1998	Lives in Aripeka, Florida and Manhattan.

"ITALIAN RIVIERA ESPRESSO CUPS," 1996, FOR ILLY ARTISTS COLLECTION.

○
STONE CRAB "IF YOU CAN GET 'EM" AND PASTA
serves 4-6

"This recipe has no garlic. At Sweets Famous Fish Restaurant at South Street in Manhattan, it is printed on the menu: 'We serve no garlic.' Personally, I love garlic, but the original ancient owners of Sweets claim it spoils fish flavor."
– *James Rosenquist*

2-3 pounds fresh stone crab claws in shell
2 large onions, chopped
1/2 pound butter
1 teaspoon fresh thyme
2 cups fresh tomato, chopped
1/2 cup red bell pepper, chopped
2 cups white wine
1 1/2 pounds spaghetti pasta

Preboil stone crab claws about 12 minutes. Take meat out of the shell. Sautè onion in butter until transluscent.

Add remaining ingredients and crab meat, and sauté together for about 5- 7 minutes. Serve hot over prepared spaghetti pasta.

> Rabbit Ridge Viognier 1996,
> Sonoma County, California

△
ARGENTINE STUFFED FLANK STEAK
Flank Steak Pocket
serves 4-6

For the Flank Steak:

2 flank steaks (1-1 1/2 pounds each)
1/2 cup dry red wine
1 tablespoon olive oil
1 small bottle prune juice

Blend ingredients and pour over steaks in a shallow non-reactie pan. Marinate overnight. Also in a separate bowl, cover the prunes with water and soak overnight.

For the stuffing:

1 tablespoon olive oil
1 garlic clove, chopped
1 teaspoon balsamic vinegar
1 cup black olives, pitted
1 cup frozen corn, thawed
1 cup frozen peas, thawed
1/4 teaspoon salt
1 cup prunes

Drain the prunes and place all of the ingredients in a pan and saute for 5 minutes without mashing. Place aside. Remove the flank steaks from the marinade and slice a large pocket into each, being careful not to puncture the sides. Save the marinade liquid. Stuff the steaks and stitch closed with cotton cord. In a skillet, sear the steaks on both sides in 2 tablespoons olive oil. Place the reserved marinade into a sauce pan and reduce it at a slow simmer to a thin syrup consistency.

Transfer the steaks to a roasting rack and roast in a preheated 325ºF oven for 30-45 minutes or until internal temperature is 125º-135ºF. Brush the reduced marinade over the steaks at intervals during cooking. Remove and allow to rest for 5 minutes. Remove the stitching, slice into halves and serve.

> Domaine Jean Grivot, Vosne-Romanée 1992,
> Burgundy, France

◇
WOLFGANG'S WHITE GRAPES
(As described by James Rosenquist)
serves 4-6

2-4 pounds seedless green grapes
1 cup sour cream
1/2 cup Cognac
1 cup brown sugar

Mix sour cream and cognac together, then mix with grapes. Transfer to a heat-proof glass container. Sprinkle with brown sugar until well covered. Place under broiler until sugar is melted. Serve.

ABOVE: "RED ONION" ACRYLIC ON CANVAS.
OPPOSITE: "PURPLE INDIAN WITH PIPE" ACRYLIC ON PAPER WITH "MOTHER'S PLAIN CAKE" IN NAMBE WARE BOWL

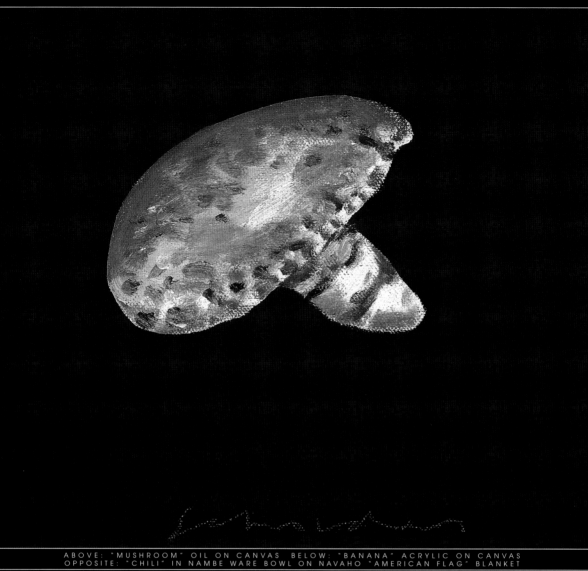

ABOVE: "MUSHROOM" OIL ON CANVAS   BELOW: "BANANA" ACRYLIC ON CANVAS
OPPOSITE: "CHILI" IN NAMBE WARE BOWL ON NAVAHO "AMERICAN FLAG" BLANKET

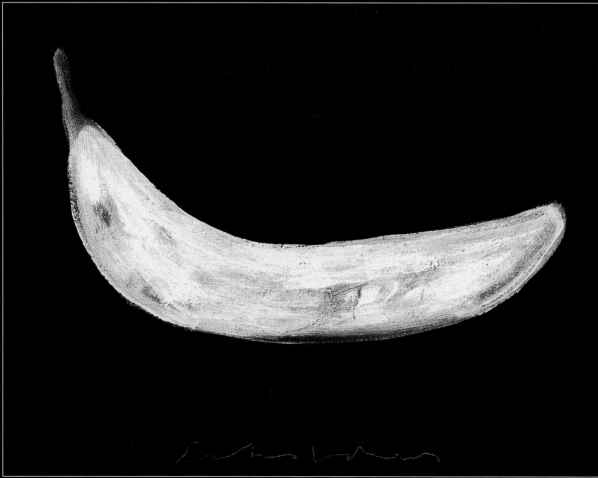

"You can't have preconceived ideas. If you know how something is going to look before you begin, there is no reason to paint it. So you walk in as open as possible and put marks on the canvas that in some way communicate. The communication should be esoteric and mysterious to the uninitiated."

1937	b. Breckenridge, MN., father employed by the Bureau of Indian Affairs.
1950	Studied under Sioux painter Oscar Howe.
1957	Received Associate of Arts degree from Sacramento City College, studied art and art history under Wayne Thiebaud.
1958	First one-man show at Sacramento City College Art Gallery.
1960	Received Bachelor of Arts degree from Sacramento City College.
1964	Received Master of Arts degree from the University of Arizona, Tuscon, AZ. Taught at Institute of American Indian Arts, Santa Fe, NM.
1967	Began "Indian," series of paintings.
1969	Traveled to Europe and saw Francis Bacon paintings at Tate Museum.
1972	Included in PBS Television documentary "Three Artists."
1973	Artist-in-Residence at Dartmouth College, Hanover, NH.
1974	One-man exhibition at "Basel V International Art Fair," Bazel, Switzerland. Traveled to Egypt.
1976	Lectured at the American Cultural Center, Paris. Printed a lithograghs at Mourlot Press. Met Claude and Paloma Picasso and Françoise Gilot.
1977	PBS "Fritz Scholder," won Gold Plaque Award, Chicago Film Festival.
1978	Produced nine oversize intagilo etchings for 2RC Editrice, Rome.
1980	Ended "Indian" series. Won "Distinguished American Indian Award," NM.
1981	Exhibited "Fritz Scholder Retrospective: 1960-1981," Tucson Museum of Art. Executed lithographs at Ediciones Poligrafa in Barcelona, Spain. Began "Dream" series.
1982	"Fritz Scholder, An American Portrait," is shown in New York. Began "Mysteries" series.
1985	"Honorary Doctorate of Fine Arts, University of Arizona, Tucson.
1989	Guest Artist, The Dakota Centennial Arts Congress, Aberdeen, SD. Exhibited at the Hermitage, Leningrad, Russia and the Himeji City Museum of Art, Japan.
1990	Honary Doctorate of Humane Letters, the College of Santa Fe, NM.
1991	Exhibited the "Human in Nature" series at the Alexander Gallery, NY.
1992	Exhibited "Man and Dog - Woman and Dog," Yares Gallery, Santa Fe, NM.
1993	Exhibited "Martyr" and "Centaur" paintings at Louis Newman Gallery, Beverly Hills, CA.
1996	Began "Fruit and Vegetable" series.
1998	Lives in Scottsdale, AZ.

"WEE DREAM HORSE" BRONZE, 1987

SCHOLDER'S CHILI
serves 4

2 lbs. lean ground beef

4 tablespoons chili powder

1 teaspoon salt

2 teaspoons cumin seeds, crushed

1 teaspoon cayenne

1 teaspoon cinnamon

2 cloves garlic, minced

3 cups cooked pinto beans

2 cups tomato sauce

2 cups diced tomatoes, canned

In a large cast iron skillet, brown ground beef and drain. Add spices. Stir in tomatoes and tomato sauce. Simmer for 30 minutes. Add beans and simmer allowing flavors to blend. Salt to taste

"FOND MEMORIES OF WOODS"
serves 4-6

2 1/2 pounds Beef tenderloin thinly sliced for medallions 1/8- to 1/4-inch thick

1/4 pound butter

4 lemons

salt

freshly ground black pepper

capers

Season beef with salt and pepper. In a large skillet, melt butter over medium heat and sauté beef about one minute each side. Squeeze juice of one lemon over medallions at the end of sautéing. Transfer to a warm serving platter.

Sprinkle with capers and serve with lemon wedges.

1-2-3 MARGARITA
The way it was invented.

1 part fresh lime juice

2 parts Cointreau

3 parts "best Tequila you can find"

Mix and enjoy!

SANGRITA (WIDOW'S BLOOD)
A non-alcoholic chaser for a margarita

1 cup fresh orange juice

1 cup tomato juice

1 lime, squeezed

1 tablespoon chile juice

2 tablespoons grenadine

1 teaspoon hot pepper sauce

1 tablespoon chopped cilantro

4 tablespoons hot salsa

Combine in a pitcher. Season with salt and pepper. Fill four glasses with ice and serve.

MY MOTHER'S PLAIN CAKE WITH NUTMEG SAUCE

Plain Cake

2 cups sifted cake flour

3 teaspoons baking powder

1/2 teaspoon salt

1 cup sugar

1/2 cup vegetable shortening

1 teaspoon vanilla extract

2 eggs

3/4 cup milk

Preheat oven to 350º F. Grease and flour one long cake pan (or two round pans).

Sift together flour, baking powder and salt. In a separate bowl, mix sugar with shortening. Add vanilla and eggs, one at a time. Add 1/4 flour mixture and beat until smooth. Add 1/2 the milk, then 1/2 the flour, then rest of milk and rest of flour, blending until smooth after each addition.

Bake for 20-25 minutes (or 20 minutes if using round pans).

NUTMEG SAUCE

2 cups boiling water

6 tablespoons sugar

1/2 teaspoon salt

2 rounded tablespoons flour

1 teaspoon ground nutmeg

3 teaspoons butter

In a small saucepan, boil water. In a mixing bowl, mix dry ingredients. Add butter and a little boiling water. Whisk to keep from lumping. Add to remaining boiling water on stove, stirring with whisk. Reduce heat and simmer, stirring occasionally. Pour sauce on cooled cake, then serve.

"SKULL" BRONZE, 1987

ABOVE: "ODETTE" CHALICE IN SILVER AND CERAMIC
OPPOSITE: "SOUP ORGY IN FOUR COLORS" WITH CERAMIC AND WOOD "SALT AND PEPPER SHAKERS"

"I'm a vagabond in the cultures of the world, but I see myself Slavonic, perhaps enigmatic, certainly romantic and sentimental. Do you understand what I mean? This sense of humor that sets you off laughing at yourself."

1949	b. Prague.
1969	Studied furniture design at the School for Arts and Crafts in Prague.
1969	Moved to Germany and studied architecture at the High School for Art in Hamburg.
1973	Studied Philosophy in Stuttgart.
1978	Scientific assistant at the Institute for Industrial Design at the University of Hannover.
1979	Graduated in architecture at the Technical University, Delft, The Netherlands.
1982	Was Lecturer in design-theory at the University of Essen.
1983	Won Honorable mention for the "German Architectural Prize" for the design of house, Sipkova, Hamburg. Moved to Amsterdam and opened architectural and design studio.
1987	Solo exhibition at the "Musee de Arts Decoratifs" in Lyon.
1989	Awarded the Kho Liang Le prize for design.
1990	Appointed Professor of Architecture at Prague Academy of Applied Art.
1991	Solo exhibition at the "Stedelijk Museum," Amsterdam. Awarded "La Croix Chevalier dana l'Ordre de Arts et des Lettres'" by the French government.
1992	Appointed as Vaclay Havel and began restoration of the Prague Castel. Solo exhibition at the "Vitra Design Museum" in Weilam Rhein, Germany.
1993	Solo exhibition at the Museum for Decorative Arts in Prague. Awarded the "Prins Bernhard Fonds Prize" for Architecture and applied art.
1994	Designed "Museum Het Kruithuis" in Den Bosch, The Netherlands. "Opera House in Kyoto," Japan. "Boutique for Karl Lagerfeld, Paris."
1996	"Apartments for Municipality of Apeldoom," The Netherlands. Designed Steltman Gallery, NYC.
1998	Lives in Amsterdam.

ENTRY: PRAGUE CASTLE; CZECH REPUBLIC

BOŘEK ŠÍPEK

FOOD FOR SOUP-ORGY IN FOUR COLOURS
Black, Red, White, and Yellow Soup.

○
BLACK (MEAT)
serves 4

2 pounds lambmeat with bone

1 quart water

1 chorizo (Spanish sausage)

2 big onions

1 pound black beans
(soaked overnight)

salt and pepper

1 tablespoon ground cumin

1 tablespoon fresh ginger root

2 or 3 mexican black peppers

Simmer all the ingredients for 1 1/2 hours on a low heat (until the beans disintegrate). Pass through sieve without stirring (do not purée) and throw away the rest.

Add the black beans and the ginger root, and cook another 10 minutes, then serve with fresh green coriander (cilantro). The meat can be served on a separate plate.

> Echézeaux, Domaine de la Romanée-Conti 1990, Côte de Nuits, France

○
RED (FISH)
serves 4

4 pounds tomatoes in pieces

4 pounds various small fish (whole)

5 big heads of fish

3 tablespoons paprika powder
(spicy)

3 big onions

5 cloves garlic

Put all ingredients in the pan, without adding any water and simmer for 1 1/2 hours. Pass through sieve and push liquid out (do not purée), throw away the rest. Serve with fresh basil and garlic croutons.

> Carmenet Sauvignon/Semillon Reserve 1995, Edna Valley, California

○
WHITE (VEGETARIAN)
serves 4

2 big carrots

1 celery root (celeriac)

2 courgettes (zucchini)

2 onions

parsley

Cook all these ingredients for 30 minutes, pass through sieve and throw away the rest.

4 young potatoes, 1/4-inch dice

caraway seed

1 quart whole milk

3 eggs

juice of 2 lemons

Add the ingredients and cook for 10 minutes. Add the unbeaten eggs, one at a time and beat vigorously. Add the lemon juice.

> Louis M. Martini Reserve Chardonnay 1994, Russian River Valley, California

○
YELLOW (POULTRY)
serves 4

1 pheasant

3 big onions

3 big whole fennel

10 pieces of cubed pumpkin
(1/2-inch size cubes)

1 teaspoon saffron

2 cloves garlic

salt

Add enough water to cover pheasant. Simmer all ingredients for 1 hour and pass through sieve, (do not purée),

Serve with small pieces of meat.

> Robert Mondavi Chardonnay 1995, Napa Valley, California

DETAIL: KARL LAGERFELD BOUTIQUE, PARIS

ABOVE/BELOW: "THE ATLANTIS" MIAMI, FLORIDA OPPOSITE: "PAELLA" IN THE "SKY COURT OF THE ATLANTIS" MIAMI, FL

"There is a precarious element in all our buildings. It has nothing to do with deconstructionism. It's about buildings exploding."

1951	b. Mayo Clinic, Rochester, MN, father a thoracic surgeon, mother feminist activist.
1968	Graduated from Everglades School for Girls, Coconut Grove, FL.
1972	Received Bachelor of Arts in Fine Arts from Brown University, Providence, RI.
1975	Received a Masters in Architecture from Columbia University, NYC.
1975	Progressive Architecture Award for Spear House with Rem Koolhaas.
1976	Married Bernardo Fort-Brescia.
1977	Founded Arquitectonica (an International Architectural Firm).
1978	Awarded Rome Prize (Prix di Roma) The American Academy in Rome.
	"Spear Residence" is constructed, Miami, FL. Progressive Architecture Award.
	"Babylon" apartments, Miami, FL.
1981	"The Palace" residential tower, Miami, FL.
1982	"The Atlantis" and "The Imperial" residential towers, Miami; "Overseas Tower" offices, Miami, FL; "Decorateve Arts Plaza," Miami, FL.
1983	"Taggart Town Houses" and "Haddon Town Houses," Houston, TX.
1985	"Mulder House," Lima, Peru; "Dade County Justice Center," Miami, FL.
1986	"Creditbank Tower," Miami, FL
1987	"Walner House," Glencoe, IL.; "Rio" Shopping Center, Atlanta, GA.
1988	"Miracle Center" Shopping complex, Miami, FL; "Banco de Credito del Peru," Lima; "Center for Innovative Technology," Herndon, VA.
1990	"Sawgrass Mills" Shopping Center, Sunrise, FL; "Washingtonian Center," Office complex, Gaithersburg, MD.
1991	ARQUITECTONICA by Beth Dunlap, (The AIA Press, Washington, DC.) "Bank of America," Beverly Hills, CA.
1995	Ran 26.2-mile New York Marathon, taught at Harvard, lectured in Japan. Won design competition for "Times Square" entertainment complex, NYC.
1996	Won design competition for "Miami Arena." Designed MTV offices, Miami, FL.
1998	Lives with husband, Bernado Fort-Brescia and their six children in Coral Gables, Florida.

PISCO SOUR

3 jiggers Pisco

2 jiggers lime juice

1 jigger sugar

1 egg white

Mix all ingredients, shake with ice. Pour in glasses, add ice on top. Top with bitters or cinnamon if desired.

MIAMI PAELLA
serves 4

8 cups chicken broth or canned chicken broth

3 tablespoons butter

1 large onion finely chopped

3 cups arborio rice

1 ounce saffron

1 red pepper, chopped fine

3 cloves garlic

2 bay leaves

2 pounds shrimp

2 pounds mussels

2 pounds steamed stone crab claws

1 pound chicken legs - bone in,

skin on cut into 3 inch pieces

1/2 bunch parsely, chopped fine

3 green onions, bias cut

Bring the chicken broth up to a boil. Remove from heat, steep the saffron in the hot stock. Melt 3 tablespoons butter in a large saucepan, when butter foams add onion and garlic. Sauté over medium heat until translucent. Add rice and mix well.

When rice is coated with butter add wine. Cook, stirring constantly until wine has evaporated. Stir in one or two ladels of saffron broth, or enough to cover rice. Stir over meduim heat until broth has been absorbed. Continue cooking and stirring rice, adding broth a little at a time, 10 minutes. During remaining 10 minutes of cooking, add bay leaf and shrimp, steamed stone crab claws and cooked chicken. Rice is done when it is tender, but firm to the bite and when all other ingredients are hot and tender. Garnish with steamed mussels, chopped red pepper, parsley and green onion.

> Carmenet Reserve Sauvignon Blanc/Semillon
> 1995, Edna Valley, California

◇

(ARROZ CON POLLO) RICE WITH CHICKEN BY SALLY FERTITTA
serves 4-6

3 fryer chickens

12 green bananas

black olives

LeSoeur peas

pimento

rice

Bermuda onion

garlic

lemon or orange juice

saffron, yellow food coloring

sherry

College Inn Chicken broth

2 cans tomato paste

Peel bananas, soak in 2 eggs with milk and dash of sherry. Keep turning them. Refrigerate if they seem out too long.

Place chickens on a platter and rub with orange or lemon juice. Press a mixture of salt, pepper and garlic onto the chickens. Put couple of pinches of saffron in bowl, mix with cold water. (Be sure it is good and new saffron.) Add cans of broth (reserving fat floating on top for later use) to saffron mixture.

Squeeze garlic clove in mixture. Add 2 teaspoons of tomato paste. Add several drops of yellow food coloring. Place margarine, oil, chicken fat (from top of College Inn can) in frying pan and brown chicken. (It has been slightly dredged with flour.)

Add onion when you turn chicken over. (Bermuda by far best). Add broth mixture. Simmer for a minute.

Rice: Pour rice under chicken, mixing rice into liquid as you do. Put aside about 1/2 cup of 1/2 water, 1/2 sherry to add to chicken to make more liquid as liquid cooks down.

Bananas Con't: Dip banana into sugar mixture. Brown bananas on medium flame. Watch them carefully so they do not become overcooked. Watch chicken. You want all the liquid absorbed. Slice pimento and black olives.

Sally says use butter to fry bananas when you have company. Hal overheard this and said,"Have none for me. I'll be out that night."

If you serve in a skillet, put peas in middle. If on platter, put all around decoratively in mounds.

Make spoke design with pimento. Scatter black olives on top. Grind pepper on top. Paprika. Put bananas around entire dish.

Serve this with black bean soup, avacodo and grapefruit salad. (Sis Samuels says Thomas bananas best.) Cuban bread. Flan with carmalized top.

Serve cold, strawberry center of wheel. White wind: Soave or orvieto or dry spanish wine. Daiqueries. Full Cuban dinner. Add clams, lobster, shrimp, corizas (spanish sausage), to dish for company.

◇

DIANE SYMONETTE'S CRÊME BRULÈE (FROM MELANIE)
serves 4-6

Leave eggs out so they become room temperature.

4 egg yolks

2 1/2 pints cream

Beat egg yolks well. Bring cream to a boil, let boil 1 minute, stir constantly. Pour cream into egg yolks, stirring. Put in double boiler. Cook and stir until it coats the back of a spoon. Pour into well buttered pyrex dish. Chill in icebox 4-5 hours.

For Topping:

1/3 cup dark brown sugar

Put under broiler with oven door open. Watch as it starts caramelizing. Turn. Return to icebox.

◇

KEY LIME PIE
Recipe for one 9" pie

Triple recipe for two 11" pies. Make pie crusts first, cool.

1 envelope plain gelatin

1/8 cup cold water

4 eggs, separated

1/2 cup lime juice

1 cup sugar

1/4 teaspoon salt

1 teaspoon lime rind

1/2 cup heavy cream, whipped

Soften gelatin in cold water. Beat egg yolks in top of double boiler.

Mix lime juice, 1/2 cup sugar and salt. Cook over hot water until mixture thickens slightly, stirring constantly. Remove from heat. Add gelatin. Stir until dissolved. Add lime rind. Beat egg whites until stiff peaks form. Gradually beat in remaining sugar. Fold gelatin mixture into egg whites. Then fold in whipped cream. Turn into cooled pie shell.

Chill for at least 2 hours, preferably overnight before serving.

ABOVE AND OPPOSITE: "FELIX RESTAURANT," THE PENINSULA HOTEL, HONG KONG   BELOW: "MAX LE CHINOIS" COLANDER FOR ALESSI

BELOW: "JO JO LONG LEG" KNIFE FOR LAGUIOLE AND "JUICY SALIF," CITRUS SQUEEZER FOR ALESSI

4 MINUTES BOILED EGGS WITH C

ANd

VIAR , WHITE TRUFFLE , URCHIN

LOVE

PHILIPPE STARCK

ARTIST

"I am not a good decorator. I have no taste. I work with semantics and symbol and around enjoyment. I want to propose a better life."

1949	b. Paris, father an inventor and aerospace engineer.
1967	Studied at École Nissim de Camondo in Paris.
1979	Founded the "Starck Product Company."
1984	"Cafe Costes," Paris, including "Costes" and "Costes Alumnio" chairs.
	"Palias de l'Ely`see," Paris; for Francois Mitterrand, "Prèsident M," Table.
1985	"Restaurant Theatron," Mexico; "Laguiole Set" Steak Knives.
1987	"Laguiole Factory," Laguiole, France.
	"Mandala Pasta," "Puzzle," Nightclub, Paris.
1988	"Cafe Mystique," Tokyo; "The Le Moult House," Paris.
	"Royalton Hotel," New York; "Lola Mundo," chair/table.
1989	"Nani Nani," office building, Tokyo.
1990	"Restaurant Teatriz," Madrid. Won "American Institute of Architects Honor Award," Royalton Hotel, NYC.
1991	STARCK® (Benedikt Taschen Verlag GmbH, Cologne).
1992	"Olympic Flame," winter Olympics, Albertville; "Louis XX," stacking chair.
1993	"Groningen Museum," Netherlands. Won the "Grand Prix National de la Creation Industrielle."
1994	"Restaurant Felix in the Peninsula Hotel," Hong Kong; "Stark House," for (3 Suisses) prefabricated, "Lord Yo," and "Oily Tango."
1995	"Delano Hotel," and "Blue Door Restaurant," Miami; "Comboo," TV and CD Player. Won "Interior Architecture Award," by Interior Design Magazine.
1996	"Mondrian Hotel," Beverly Hills; "Placido Arango Jr. House," Madrid. "Ego," Video recorder; "Fuga," portable CD player; "Eyeglasses," or Mikli. STARCK (Benedikt Taschen Verlag GmbH, Cologne).
1998	Lives in Paris and 9 homes around the world.

4 MINUTES BOILED EGGS WITH CAVIAR, WHITE TRUFFLE, URCHIN AND LOVE

BONJOUR

A LUMINESCENT WARM WHITE BACKGROUND.
SOME CAVIAR, THE WHITE TRUFFLE, A
SEA URCHIN, 3 EGGS, A STAINLESS STEEL
PAN (~~OR SILVER BUT WITH CLEAN SHAPE~~)
A LITTE SPOON A SPECIAL EFFECT TO HAVE
JUST THE BLUE GAZ FLAME LIKE THAT: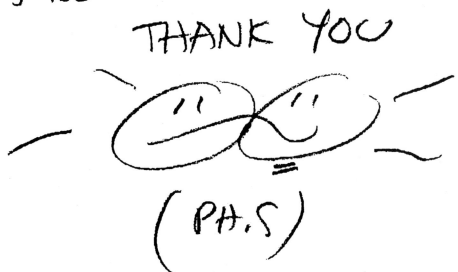
OR LIKE THAT :
BUT JUST THE FLAME
AND A PRINT OF STRONG RED LIPSTICK
WOMEN MOUTH.
ALL THAT PRESENT LIKE THE DESIGN.
THAT'S ALL

THANK YOU

(PH.S)

ABOVE: "THE MUSEUM OF MODERN ART" NYC OPPOSTIE: "FRIED CHICKEN, CRISP SLAW, BROILED GRAPEFRUIT, HARD
BOILED QUAIL EGGS AND LEMONADE" AT UNIVERSITY OF ARKANSAS "MARRIED STUDENT HOUSING," FAYETTEVILLE, AR

"The overhanging eaves were a departure from the international style, which placed the glass on the surface of the building unprotected from the sun and I adopted this principle in all subsequent buildings."

1902	b. Fayetteville, Arkansas, mother a professor of English, father a Yale educated merchant.
1923	Studied Architecture at the University of Arkansas, Fayetteville, AR.
1925	Studied Architecture, Harvard, Boston, MA.
1926	Studied Architecture, MIT, Cambridge, MA.
1935	Worked on design and development of Rockefeller Center, NYC.
1939	"Goodyear House", Old Westburg, Long Island, NY
	"Museum of Modern Art" with Philip Goodwin, Panama.
1946	"El Panama Hotel", Panama City, Panama.
1954	"Untied States Embassy", New Delhi, India.
1955	"Gold Medal" The American Institute of Architects.
1957	"United States Pavilion", Brussels World Fair, Belgium.
	"University of Arkansas Married Student Housing", Fayetteville, AR.
1958	"Gallery of Modern Art" for Huntington Hartford, NYC.
1960	"Resident Architect," The American Academy in Rome.
1961	"Perpetual Savings and Loan Association", Beverly Hills, CA.
1962	THE EVOLUTION OF AN ARCHITECT by Ed Stone (Horizon Press, NY)
1964	"National Geographic Society Headquarters", Washington, DC.
1966	"Busch Memorial Stadium", St. Louis, MO.
1968	"General Motors Building", NYC.
1971	"John F. Kennedy Center for the Performing Arts", Washington, DC.
1973	"Pepsico World Headquarters", Purchase, KY.
1974	"Standard Oil Building and Plaza", Chicago, IL.
1978	d. New York City, NY.

"GALLERY OF MODERN ART," NYC

SOUTHERN FRIED CHICKEN
serves 4

2 frying chickens (approximately 2-2 1/2 pounds each)

1/2 cup all-purpose flour

1 1/2 teaspoons salt

3/4 teaspoon pepper

enough vegetable oil to deep fry

Wash chicken and cut into serving pieces. Put flour salt and pepper into paper bag. Add chicken, close top and shake. Heat oil to 370ºF. Slowly put 3 to 4 pieces of chicken into hot oil and fry until golden brown and tender (approximately 15 minutes). Drain, keep warm in oven until all pieces are fried. Have a great feed! Leftovers are good served cold.

> Negra Modelo, Mexico with fresh Lime

MARY'S CRISPY SLAW
serves 4

1 head red or green cabbage

1/4 cup red wine vinegar

1/2 cup vegetable oil

1/2 teaspoon salt
and 1/4 teaspoon pepper

garlic powder

Shred a small head of red or green cabbage as fine as possible, (chiffonade). Mix vinegar, oil, salt, pepper and garlic powder and toss with cabbage, then allow to chill in refrigerator for at least one hour.

BLACK EYED PEAS
serves 2-4

1/2 pound dried black-eyed peas, picked over

1 medium onion, chopped

1 teaspoon finely chopped garlic

1 teaspoon dried thyme, crumbled

1 bay leaf

4 strips smoked bacon, quartered

In a 3- to 4- quart sauce pan simmer peas and enough water to cover by 2 inches until tender, 50 minutes to an hour. While peas are cooking, in a large heavy skillet cook bacon and onion over moderately low heat, stirring occasionally, until bacon is cooked. Add garlic, thyme, and bay leaf and cook, stirring, 1 minute (add bacon mixture to cooked peas. Discard bay leaf and season with salt and pepper.

BLINI
serves 8

1 cup buttermilk, yogurt or light sour cream

1 cup buckwheat pancake mix

1 egg yolk

1 tablespoon melted butter

To serve 8 as a first course stir one cup buttermilk, yogurt or light sour cream into a cup of buckwheat pancake mix. add the well-beaten yolk of an egg, 1 tablespoon melted butter. Beat thoroughly. Allow to stand uncovered at room temperature at least ten minutes or until ready to use. Fold in stiffly beaten egg white. Drop by tablespoons on well-greased griddle, cook on high heat until covered with pinpoints or until golden brown. Turn and cook other side. Serve as an appetizer with sour cream and caviar.

SPOON BREAD
serves 4

1 cup yellow corn meal

1 1/2 teaspoon salt

1 cup cold milk

2 cups scalded milk

2 well beaten eggs

3 tablespoons melted butter

Mix and stir until smooth, corn meal, salt and milk. Add above mixture to 2 cups scalded milk (do not boil). Stir constantly over flame until thick (about 5 minutes). Add thickened mixture slowly to the beaten eggs Blend well. Add melted butter. Blend. Pour into well buttered 1 1/2 quart baking dish. Bake in 350ºF oven for 50 min. Serve immediately.

BROILED GRAPEFRUIT
serves 4

Slice grapefruit in half, top half with 1/4 inch brown sugar, place on cookie sheet under high broiler until sugar melts . . . serve immediately.

LEMONADE
4 quarts

6 lemons

4 quarts water, 2 cups reserved

2 cups sugar

extra lemons for garnish

In a heavy-bottomed non-reactive sauce pot heat the 2 cups water with the sugar until the sugar dissolves. Cool. Add the remaining water. Cut lemons in half, squeeze out all the juice. Add to sugar water mixture in a large pitcher. Slice lemons and add for garnish.

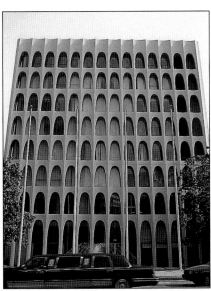

"PERPETUAL SAVINGS," BEVERLY HILLS, CA

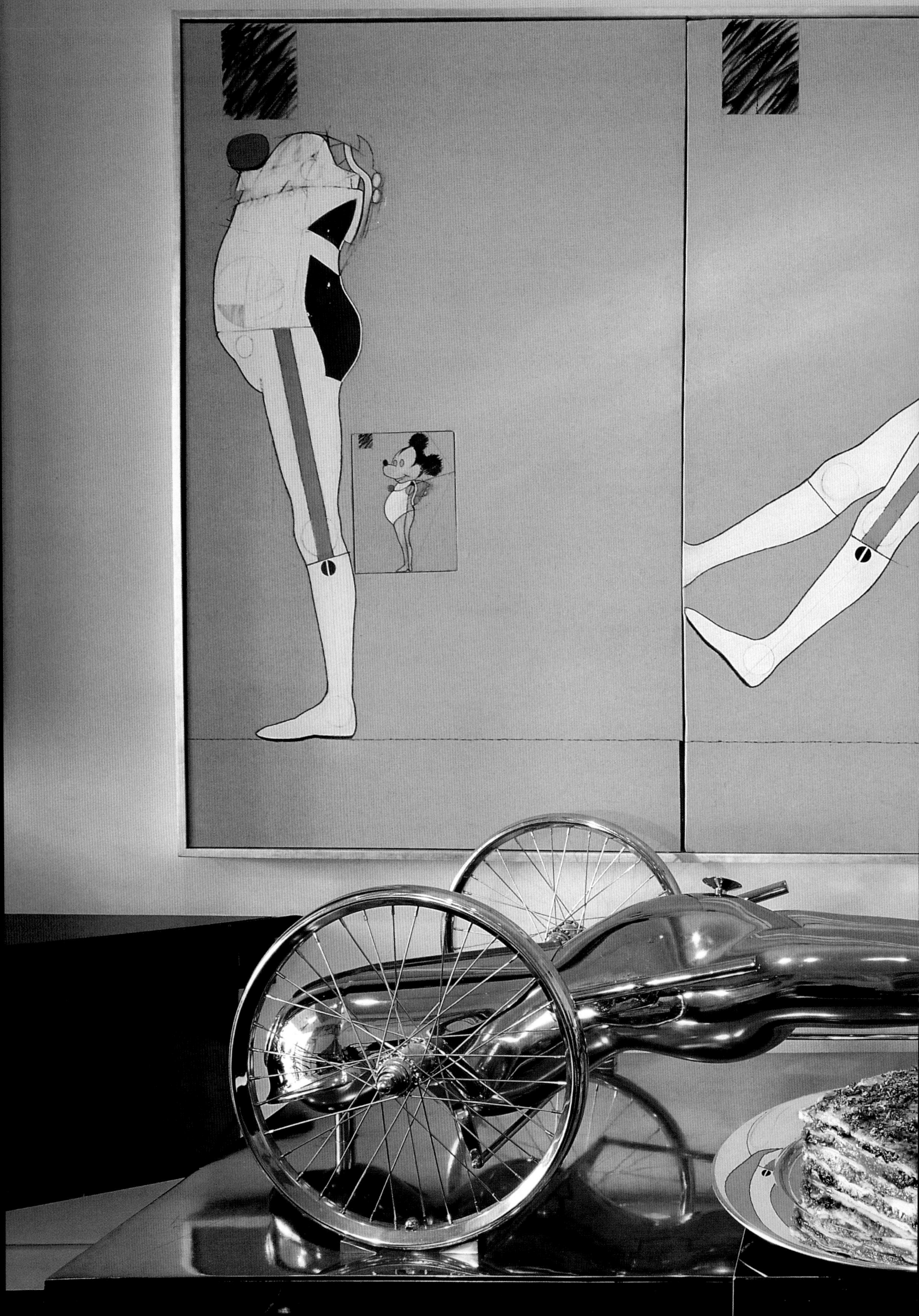

"Fortunate man has the unique ability of 'laughing' therapeutically at himself when confronted with absurdness in the world he inherited. The next step for the rational man is to construct a system which will enable him to cope with these absurdities."

1927	b. Ernest Tino Trova, St. Louis, Missouri, father an industrial designer.
1944	Created drawings and watercolors (self-taught).
1947	"Roman Boy," painting published in Life Magazine, Exhibition at St. Louis Art Museum, St. Louis, MO.
1949	Visited Ezra Pound at St. Elizabeth's Hospital, Washington, DC.
1950	Wrote poetry for his magazine "Moat," which included work of Ezra Pound.
1952	Joined U.S. Army Special Services, Fort Benning, GA.
1953	Traveled to New York and met Willem DeKooning.
1959	First solo exhibition, "Image Gallery," St. Louis, MO.
1960	Married Carla Clingman Rand. Painted to the accompaniment of a jazz group on stage of the Crystal Palace, St. Louis, MO. Designed stage setting for play, "Samuel Beckett."
1961	Began "Falling Man," series of paintings and sculptures.
1963	Executed Formica paintings and sculptures: sculptures in clay and plaster; fiberglass sculptures; kinetic sculptures. One-man show held in May Company Department Store, St. Louis, MO.
1965	"Trovascope," commissioned by the Museum of Modern Art, NY. (Second version 1974).
1969	Created "Trova/Index," 40 items including a watch, coins, bronze ring and 6" hinged man.
1970	Created paper graphic sculpture for Playboy Magazine.
1972	Began Profile Canto Series of Sculptures in Cor-ten Steel.
1973	ARTIST SLAIN, by Ernest Trova (2:30 Productions, NY).
1976	St. Louis County opened Laumeier Sculpture Park with 40 Trova Sculptures.
1979	Received "The National Humanitarian Award," by National Recreation and Park Association.
1981	Created Stainless Steel Sculpture for "Council of Fashion Designers of America Award." Exhibited "Poet Series," NY.
1983	Received the "Utsukushi-ga-hara Open Air Museum Award," Tokyo, Japan. Exhibited "Iglesian/Troubadour," series, Miami, FL.
1984	Began "Etc/Troubadour," series.
1986	Opened "Trova Studio," in St. Louis, MO.
1987	TROVA, by Udo Kultermann and Andrew Kagan (Abrams, NY). Began "Seated Man," series.
1988	Created "The Journey," a monumental stainless steel fountain.
1998	Lives with wife Carla in Clayton, Missouri.

ABOVE: "FALLING MAN WRIST WATCH," FROM "TROVA/INDEX" PREVIOUS TWO PAGES: "LASAGNA" WITH "STUDY/FALLING MAN TRIPTYCH (WITH FALLING MOUSE) ACRYLIC ON CANVAS" AND "STUDY/FALLING MAN(CARMAN) POLISHED BRONZE AND ENAMEL

LASAGNE
serves 4-6

1 pound lasagne noodles

1 quart spaghetti sauce with meat

1 pound Italian sausage

1 cup water

15 oz. ricotta cheese

1 egg beaten

8 ounces shredded mozzarella

1/3 cup water

1/4 cup parmesan cheese

3 tablespoons fresh
chopped parsley

dash nutmeg

salted garlic Italian seasoning and
pepper to taste

1/2 cup parmesan cheese

4 large garlic cloves pressed
or chopped fine

Preheat oven to 375ºF. Brown sausage in saucepan. Drain fat. Add 1 quart spaghetti sauce, 1 cup water and garlic. Bring to boil.

In large bowl, mix ricotta cheese, beaten egg, mozzarella cheese, 1/3 cup water, 1/4 cup parmesan cheese, parsley, nutmeg and salted Italian seasoning.

To arrange:
Use lasagne strips uncooked, but rinse in hot water, then layer in a 9-x13-x4-inch pan. (Approximately 4 lasagne strips will fit in the pan for a single layer - 3 lengthwise and 1 crosswise).

For Layering:
1 2/3 cup sauce, lasagne strips, 1/2 cheese mixture, then 1 2/3 cup sauce, lasagne strips, remaining sauce, top with 1/2 cup parmesan cheese.

Bake at 375Fº covered with aluminum foil for 40 minutes. Remove foil and bake for 15 minutes longer. Important: let stand for 5 to 10 minutes before cutting.

Justin Isosceles Reserve 1992,
San Louis Obispo County, California

SUNFLOWER (HELIANTHUS ANNUUS)
PANSY (VIOLA X WITTROCKIANA)
HOLLYHOCK (ALCEA ROSEA)
DANDELION (TARAXACUM OFFICINALE)

NASTURTIUM (TROPAEOLUM MAJUS)
TULIP (TULIPA)
DAYLILY (HEMEROCALLIS FULVA)
BORAGE (BORAGO OFFICINALIS)

YUCCA (YUCCA FILAMENTOSA)
HIBISCUS (HIBISKOS MALLOW)
ROSE (ROSA)
SIGNET MARIGOLD (TAGETES SIGNATA)

EAT ONLY ORGANICALLY GROWN FLOWERS/REMOVE STAMENS. EAT IN MODERATION

"I like complexity and contradiction in architecture… based on the richness and ambiguity of modern experience, including that experience which is inherent in art."

1925	b. Philadelphia, Pennsylvania.
1947	Received Bachelor of Architecture, Princeton University, NJ.
1950	Received Masters in Architecture, Princeton University, NJ.
1953	Worked for Eero Saarinen and Associates, CT.
1956	Awarded the "Rome Prize in Architecture," (Prix de Roma) The American Academy in Rome.
1966	"Resident Architect of the American Academy in Rome," " Fire Station No. 4," Columbus, IN, "COMPLEXITY AND CONTRADICTION IN ARCHITECTURE by Robert Venturi (Museum of Modern Art, New York).
1967	"Grands Restaurant," Philadelphia, PA.
1973	"Allen Memorial Art Museum," Oberlin, OH.
1975	"House in Vail," Vail, CO; "House in Bermuda," Tuckers Town, Bermuda.
1979	"Furniture Design," Knoll International, NY.
1980	"Gordon Wuttall," Princeton University, Princeton, NJ.
1987	VENTURI, RAUCH, AND SCOTT BROWN: BUILDINGS AND PROJECTS, (Rizzoli, New York).
1989	Designed "Obects" for Swid Powell and Company, NY.
1992	"Memorial Hall," Havard University, Cambridge, MA, "Regional Government Bldg.," Toulouse, France, Kirifuri Resort Facilities," Nikko, Japan. THE EVOLUTION OF VANNA VENTURI'S HOUSE IN CHESTNUT HILL by Frederic Schwartz, (Rizzoli Int., NY.).
1998	Lives with his wife Denise Scott Brown in Philadelphia, Pennsylvania.

Very simply, Denise and I are happy vegetarians who occasionally eat fish but focus on beans, rice, fruits, vegetables and olive oil. Our favorite cuisines are peasant-like... Italian and Mexican, and we newly have come to love Japanese food.

– Robert Venturi

△

P A N S Y   P A S T A
serves 6-8

1 cup all-purpose flour

3 cups semolina flour

6 eggs (beaten)

pansies

1/2 teaspoon salt

Add the flours and salt to a food processor and combine. While processing, slowly add the oil. Continue processing until the mixutre forms a single mass. Remove and knead for approximately 5 minutes on a lightly floured surface. Add more semolina flour if needed so dough is not sticky. Cover and refrigerate for 2 or 3 hours. Roll dough through a pasta machine until very thin.

Lay out the thin dough putting half the mixture gently to the side. Arrange flower petals on the dough as desired and cover with the remaining pasta. Run very carefully through the machine one last time. Cut into strips and boil until tender (approximately 1-2 minutes). In a skillet add 2 tablespoons of exta virgin olive oil with 2 fresh garlic cloves (sliced), saute until cloves are transparent but not browned. Toss with prepared pasta and salt to taste. Garnish with fresh flower petals and herbs.

△

P A N S Y   R A V I O L I   S O U P
serves 6-8

For Vegetable Stock:

3 large carrots, peeled and small dice

2 heads celeriac (celery root), peeled and small dice

1 bunch leeks, split lenghwise, washed and medium sliced

3 purple top turnnips, peeled and small dice

3 heads garlic, split in half

10 sprigs fresh thyme

4 quarts water

In a large stock pot, combine all ingredients and water. Bring to a boil over midium high heat and simmer for at least 2 hours.

Strain and discard all the ingredients leaving only the broth. Season with salt to taste.

For Ravioli Stuffing:

1 cup ricotta cheese

1/2 cup shredded mozzarella

1/2 cup freshly grated parmesan cheese

2 eggs

1 pound fresh mushrooms, chopped, (shiitake, portobello, porcini or oyster)

2 tablespoons olive oil

2 tablespoons fresh parsley, chopped

1/2 teaspoon salt

1/2 teaspoon black pepper

Combine the cheeses in a medium bowl. Add the eggs, pasley, salt and pepper.

In a skillet, saute the mushrooms in the olive oil until soft.

Allow to cool then add to the above mixture. Set aside.

Prepare the same as the pasta recipe except when adding the flowers, place on top of each a spoon of filling.

Be sure to allow enough room between fillings to cut.

Paint water between mounds of filling and place the second sheet of pasta on top.

With a ravioli cutter or a sharp knife, cut raviolis into squares. Make sure the edges are sealed tightly. Place raviolis on a lightly floured surface.

Bring the vegetable broth to a boil and gently add the raviolis. Boil until tender (about 5 minutes).

Remove from heat and serve with broth. Garnish with pansy petals.

Caymus "Barrel Fermented" Sauvignon Blanc 1996, Napa Valley, California

ABOVE: "HELLER 'MAX' STACKING DINNERWARE" OPPOSITE: "PATES D'AMOUR" IN "COLORSTONE DINNERWARE" FOR SASKI ON
"METAFORA 1 COFFEE TABLE" FOR CASIGLIANI GLASSES BY RICHARD MEIER FOR SWID POWELL, AUDIO CABINET BY JAMES LAMBETH

"We use the contrast of scale, imaginative lighting, unusual materials, and rarefied spaces to create an environmental experience of elegance, strength and timeless values."

1933	b. Milan, Italy.
1951	Studied Architecture in Milan and Venice.
1957	Traveled to the United States on fellowships from Towle Silversmiths in Massachusetts, and the Institute of Design, Illinois Institute of Technology, Chicago.
1960	Vignelli Office of Design and Architecture was formed in Milan, Italy with wife Lella.
1964	Awarded "Gran Premio Triennale di Milano;" Designed "Stendig Calendar;" Awarded "Compasso d'Oro," by the Italian Association for Industrial Design.
1965	Moved to the United States and became the co-founder and design director of Unimark International Corporation in Chicago.
1967	Designed "Heller Stacking Dinnerware," corporate image for "Knoll International." Designed "American Airlines" logo.
1971	Established with his wife Lella, Vignelli Associates, NYC.
1973	Awarded the "Industrial Arts Medal of the American Institute of Architecture."
1975	Designed "Heller Glass Bakeware;" Designed "St. Peter's Church," logo, NYC. Designed "BMW Traveling Auto Show;" "Saks Fifth Avenue," image, NYC.
1979	Designed "Metalfora I Coffee Table," for Casigliani.
1980	Designed "TaraTable," for Rosenthal; Exhibited designs at Parsons School of Design, NY.
1983	"Handkerchief Chair," for Knoll International.
1984	"Artemide Showroom," Dallas, TX; "Cinzano Corporate Identity Program;" "Barneys," interiors and packaging, NYC; "IBM," Image program.
1986	Received first United States Presidential Design Award, President Reagan.
1987	"Artmide Showroom," Chicago, IL; "Untied States Post Office Identity," design included interior/exterior and graphics; "Palio Restaurant," NYC.
1988	"Poltrona Frau Exhibition Space," Tolentino, Italy.
1989	"Xerox Corporate Identity Program;" "Aetna Life Identity Program."
1990	DESIGN: VIGNELI (Rizzoli International Publications, Inc.).
1998	Lives with wife Lella in New York City.

PATES D'AMOUR
serves 2

4 tablespoons of olive oil

2 cloves of garlic,
peeled and smashed

dried Italian chile peppers
(1 or 2 pods, to taste)

1 package of "fresh" linguine
(supermarket brand
such as Contadina®)

1-8 ounce can of chicken broth

4 tablespoons of finely chopped
Italian parsley

salt

grated parmesan cheese

Place the olive oil, garlic and hot pepper in a skillet and heat on medium stove until the garlic is golden brown. Remove the garlic. Add the raw linguine and stir gently for a few seconds. Start adding the broth a little at a time. Wait for most of the broth to be absorbed before adding more, as you would when making a risotto. When all the broth is absorbed, but not dry, stir in the chopped parsley. Add salt to taste if necessary, sprinkle each serving with one tablespoon of grated parmesan cheese.

Buon Appetito e Buon Amore!

Cain Five 1994, Napa Valley, California

"HELLER GLASS BAKEWARE"

"The most beautiful thing in Tokyo is McDonalds.

The most beautiful thing in Stockholm is McDonalds.

The most beautiful thing in Florence is McDonalds.

Peking and Moscow don't have anything beautiful yet."

1975

1928	b. Andrew Warhola, Pittsburgh, Pennsylvania, parents immigrants from Czechoslovakia, father a construction worker, mother a maid.
1949	Received Bachelor of Fine Art, Carnegie Tech, Pittsburg, PA. Exhibited at Carnegie Gallery.
1950	Moved to New York City, Won "Art Directors Club Medal," for his illustrations.
1952	First Solo Exhibition "Fifteen Drawings Based on the Writings of Truman Capote," Hugo Gallery, NY. Illustrated Amy Vanderbilt's COMPLETE BOOK OF ETIQUETTE, (Doubleday, New York).
1956	Work exhibited in Museum of Modern Art, NYC. Designed with Suzie Frankfort.
1962	Began "Elizabeth Taylor," "Elvis Presley," "Soup Can," and "Marilyn Monroe" Paintings. Made films; "Eat," "Batman," "Dracula," "Couch," "Empire," and "Harlot."
1966	Exhibited "Cow" wallpaper and "Silver Clouds," at Leo Castelli Gallery, NYC.
1967	Exhibited "Self Portrait," at U.S. Pavilion in Expo '67, Montreal, Canada. ANDY WARHOL'S INDEX (Random House, New York), SCREEN TESTS/ A DIARY (Kulchur Press, NYC).
1968	Warhol was shot by Valerie Solanas. Solo exhibition in Stockholm, Oslo, Bern, and Ameterdam.
1969	Created "Interview," magazine. Solo exhibition, National Galerie, Berlin.
1971	Album cover design "Sticky Fingers," for Rolling Stones, received Grammy Award Nomination.
1973	Appeared in the film "The Drivers Seat," with Elizabeth Taylor.
1975	THE PHILOSOPHY OF ANDY WARHOL (FROM A TO B AND BACK AGAIN), (Jovanovich Press, NYC).
1976	Began "Skull," "Hammer and Sickle," paintings.
1977	Frequented Studio 54 with friends Halston, Bianca Jagger and Liza Minnelli.
1980	Began "Shoe" paintings, developed "Andy Warhol's TV," television series. Traveled to Rome and had audience with Pope John Paul I.
1982	The Castelli Gallery exhibited "Dollar Sign" paintings. Traveled to Hong Kong and Beijing.
1983	Began painting with Jean-Michel Basquiat and Francesco Celemente. Appeared in a Japanese TV commercial for TDK videotape.
1984	Began "Rorschach" paintings.
1985	Signed Keith Haring's "Andy Mouse" series. Began to be represented by Ford Modeling Agency, painted "Absolut Vodka,"
1986	Began "Last Supper" and "Camoflage" paintings, appeared in "The Love Boat."
1987	d. New York City, New York.

"I know good cooks who'll spend days finding fresh garlic and fresh basil and fresh tarragon, etc., and then use canned tomatoes for the sauce, saying it doesn't matter. But I know it does matter."

△

PUMPKIN SEED-CRUSTED RED SNAPPER WITH WATERMELON

Serves 2

1-2 1/2 pounds fresh red snapper,
head and tail on

---

1 cup toasted pumpkin seeds,
rough chopped

---

1 cup corn starch

---

2 eggs, beaten

---

peanut oil for frying

---

salt and pepper to taste

---

2 slices ripe watermelon

In a heavy-bottomed non-reactive sauce pot, heat enough peanut oil to cover the whole snapper to 350ºF. Using a sharp knife, cut 3 or 4 vertical slits down both sides of the snapper. Season the snapper inside and out with salt and pepper. Roll the fish in the corn starch to cover entirely. Dip in the beaten egg to coat. Dredge fish in chopped pumpkin seeds and carefully submerge in the hot oil. Fry for 12 to 15 minutes or until cooked to desired doneness. Remove carefully from oil and let drain on paper towels. Serve warm with fresh watermelon or a fruit salsa.

> Jordan "J" Sparkling 1993,
> Alexander Valley, California

©1998 ANDY WARHOL FOUNDATION FOR THE VISUAL ARTS/ARS, NEW YORK

SELF PORTRAIT "FRIGHT WIG" 1986

"To give pleasure to man."

1919	b. Copenhagen, Denmark.
1940	Educated at the Royal Academy of Fine Arts, Copenhagen, Denmark.
1945	Exhibited his first one-man show of paintings, Denmark.
1946	Founded his ceramic workshops in Kongens Lyngloy, Denmark.
1947	Began "Poster" designs.
1957	Joined Rosenthal China Co. to create porcelain, ceramics, crystal and silver works of art.
1968	"Oding" by Jean Girandoux, designed sets and costumes for Det Ny Theatyer, Tivoli.
1971	"Wiinblad Haus" restored a group of 18th century houses containing his designs, Copenhagen. Designed dinnerware for the 2,500 year anniversary of the dynasty in Iran. Designed "Tour Des Couleurs" tapestries for Anatole Hotel, Dallas, TX.
1973	Unveiled the "Scheherezade" tapestries in the Apparel Mart, Dallas, TX.
1975	"The Four Cardinal Points," Wiinblad - Art - Furniture.
1976	"Knighted" in the order of Dannebrog by Her Majesty, The Queen of Denmark.
1977	Opened "Wiinblad Haus" in the Anatole Hotel, Dallas, TX.
1980	Awarded the President's Gold Medal for design, Italy.
1981	"The Lady and the Fool," by John Cranko, set and costume design, Royal Danish Ballet, Copenhagen, Denmark.
1983	Wrote and illustrated children's book.
1984	Designed sets and costumes for musicals "No, No Nanette" and "Around the World in Eighty Days."
1985	Shakespeare's "The Tempest" designed set for Dallas Theatre Center, Dallas, TX.
1987	"The Nutcracker," set and costume design, Dallas Ballet, Dallas, TX.
1994	"Restaurant Wiinblad," D'Angleterre, Copenhagen, Denmark.
1998	Lives in Copenhagen, Denmark, and Lausanne, Switzerland.

"RESTAURANT WIINBLAD," MENU, D'ANGLETERRE HOTEL COPENHAGEN, DENMARK

PREVIOUS TWO PAGES: "POTATO SOUP WITH CAVIAR" ON GRILL TABLE, TABLEWARE, CRYSTAL, AND STAINLESS WARE FOR ROSENTHAL. CHAIRS BY TURNER AND ROSENTHAL OF GERMANY DECORATIVE TABLE ACCESSORIES FOR BJORN WIINBLAD HAUS, COPENHAGEN AND DALLAS

△
POTATO SOUP

serves 6-8

4 medium baking potatoes
(peeled and chopped)

---

4 leeks (without greens)

---

2 tablespoons sweet butter

---

salt to taste

---

1 cup milk (brought to a boil)

---

1 egg

Chop leeks and brown them slightly in 1 tablespoon butter. Put potatoes and leeks in a medium sized pot. Add enough water to cover mixture and 1 tablespoon salt. Cover pot and cook on medium until done.

Blend mixture in a food processor until smooth, adding milk. Now add enough water to the mixture to make soup of proper consistancy. Bring to boil. Remove from heat. Beat the egg and then add a small amount of the soup to the egg, stirring constantly. Add egg to soup pot and 1 tablespoon butter and mix well. Serve hot or cold. Garnish with sliced cucumber, chives, and crème fraîche (p125) or sour cream.

Aquavit or
Far Niente Chardonnay 1995, Napa Valley, CA

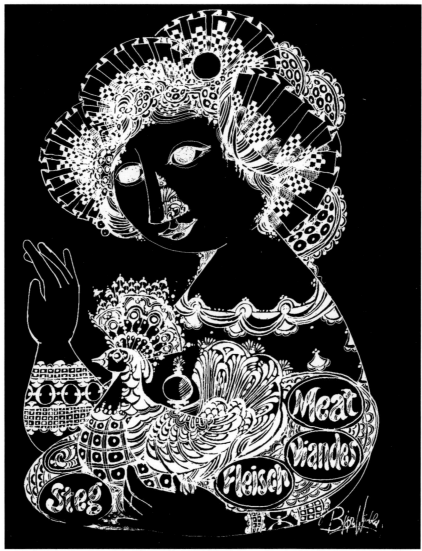

"RESTAURANT WIINBLAD" DESIGNS, D'ANGLETERRE HOTEL COPENHAGEN, DENMARK

ABOVE: "HIGHWAY 86", VANCOUVER, B.C. CANADA (SITE)
BELOW: "STREET GLASS NECKLACE" (KRIZ KIZAK) OPPOSTIE: "TAMALE PIE, WALNUT ROQUEFORT SALAD, BERRY TRIFLE"

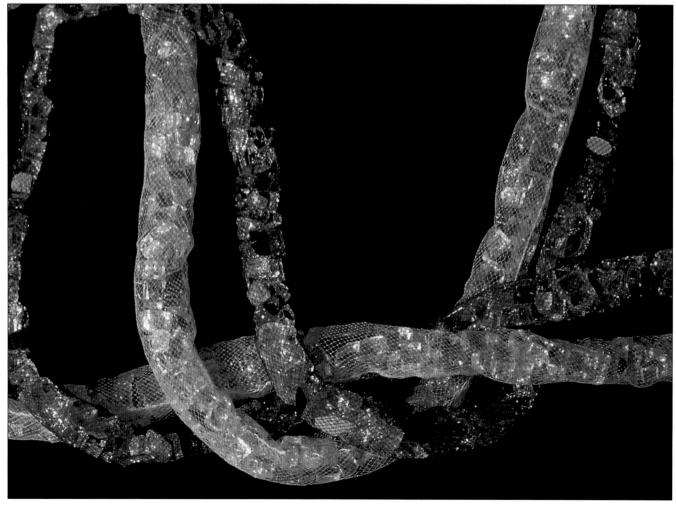

"In terms of general objectives, we're increasingly committed to the socialogical and psychological content of architecture, as opposed to problem-solving technology-- or, described another way, architecture as art, rather than architecture as design." – JAMES WINES

1932	b. James Wines. Oak Park, Illinois.
1956	Bachelor of Art and History, Syracuse University, Syracuse, NY.
	Awarded "The Rome Prize" (Prix di Roma) The American Academy in Rome.
1958	Awarded "Pulitzer Prize." Worked as a sculptor in Rome.
1962	Awarded "Guggenheim Foundation Fellowship."
1964	Awarded "Ford Foundation Grant."
1970	Founded "SITE," an architectural/landscape art design firm.
1971	"Design Award," Iron and Steel Institute.
1974	Professor at New York University.
	"Best Products Company," Houston, TX.
1982	"Willi Wear Women's Showroom," New York City, NY.
1984	Chairman, Parson's School of Design, Enivronmental Design and Architecture.
1987	DE-ARCHITECTURE by James Wines (Rizzoli, New York).
1989	SITE by Herbert Muschamp (Rizzoli, New York).
1992	"Ross's Landing Park and Plaza," Chattanooga, TN.
	"Children's Park," Toyama, Japan; "Saudi Arabian Pavilion" and
	"Avenue Number Five," at the Seville World Expo, Spain.

"By using discarded materials found in the streets of Manhattan and integrating them with illusionary fragments of nature, I have developed a form of body adornment that allows the wearer to become a personal communicator on ecological awareness." – KRIZ WINES

1950	b. Kriz Kizak.
1972	Studied art at the Cleveland Institute of Art, OH.
1974	Studied art at Georgia State Univeristy, Atlanta, GA.
1982	Studied art at the Oregon School of Arts and Crafts, OR.
1985	Founded ECOWEAR - Artwear from recycled materials.
1986	HB Studio (Dramatic Studies), NYC.
1987	Studied at the New School, NYC.
1998	Lives with husband James Wines in New York City.

When we travel in Italy, my husband, James Wines, is known among friends as an enthusiastic "Mangiatiore." In this capacity he is clearly a critic, not a chef. The best evidence of this is provided by his daughter whose only memory of her father's culinary art was when, during her childhood, James frequently prepared hot dogs for lunch which she and her little friends found rather tasty until it was discovered one day that his oddly "crunchy" wieners has always been broiled and served without removing the cellophane wrap. Since then, he eats and critiques, and allows others to mince, measure, and sauté. My involvement began when I started to fix dinner for him at his studio, because he was on crutches for six months after a serious bone fusion operation, and it was difficult for him even to manuever well enough to get to a restaurant. This progressed to his persuasions to fix "a little something" for fiends and clients who would stop by in the evening. Next, when some Italian friends came to town, he told me to organize a little dinner party -- for more than a hundred people! The clincher in our relationship whas when six Frenchmen worked at the SITE offices in New York for the summer, on a project with as tight deadline. Four of them didn't speak English, and their gastronomical taste was demanding, to say the least. I fixed lunch the first day out of hospitality, but it soon became clear that the office was a disaster zone when our foreign team members tried to get their own lunch at odd times. For the sake of organization and convenience, I started fixing "charrette" meals for fifteen people, everyday for six weeks. It kept the team together and lunchtime became a break for relaxation, sharing opinions about the project, and general socializing. We often asked outside guests to join us. During that time, I learned to budget and plan ahead, but I also found a few recipes that were worth repeating, as they were easy to make, and were well-received. Even the "mangiatore" would occasionally compliment me on the following recipes: – Kriz Kizak

TAMALE PIE
serves 8-10

There are no tamales in this: it is the generic name for a family recipe; I make my own variations, to taste. This recipe will serve at least eight, from a 9-x13-inch baking dish. It can be multiplied to serve dozens and can be prepared even a day ahead of time. The cooked dish keeps well and can be frozen to use as extra party food at a later date.

1-2 pounds of ground meat

1 uncooked hot Italian sausage

1 large eggplant (optional)

3 medium onions

8-12 plum tomatoes

3 bell peppers (red, green & yellow)

1 pound sharp cheddar cheese

1 can of corn

1 can of tomato paste

1 can of crushed tomatoes

1 can of cannelini (white beans)

1 can frijoles negros (black beans)

1 can of dark red kidney beans

1 can of diced green chiles

1 can of pitted black olives

chili power, salt, pepper to taste

1 large container of sour cream

For cornbread topping:

1 cup yellow corn meal

1/2 cup all-purpose flour

2 teaspoons baking powder

1 tablespoon sugar

dash of salt

1 egg

1 cup milk

2 tablespoons melted butter

There are a lot of ingredients, but this recipe is very simple. Sauté the meat, breaking the sausage into one inch pieces. Dice the onions, and add to the meat as it is browing, dice the peppers, reserving one quarter of each to use as decoration, and saute with the rest for a few minutes. Drain. Place in large mixing bowl. Dice and add the tomatoes. Add the crushed tomatoes and tomato paste. Drain and slice the olives, reserving some for decoration. Drain the liquid form the other ingredients, mix everything together, seasoning with chile powder (I like it spicy so I throw in a handful), salt to taste, and pour into deep baking dish.(approximately 9-x13-inch). Grate the cheese, and layer over the dish. For the cornbread topping, sift and mix the flour, add the corn meal, beat in the egg, milk, and butter. Drop in spoonfulls over the entire mixture, spreading it to create a "canvas" for decorating creatively with thin slices of the tri-color bell pepper and black olives. Bake in a 400ºF oven for about twenty minutes, or until the cornbread is done. James prefers it slightly undercooked, so the cornbread bleeds into the mixture, this can be done by broiling it, but means you must stand next to the stove to keep testing it! When serving a large group, I usually double or triple all ingredients, making at least one vegetarian version by substituting eggplant for the meat. Simply dice the eggplant, beautiful purple skin and all, sauté in olive oil, adding onions, etc. as in the regular recipe. When ready, cut into squares, serve with a salad.

> Bonny Doon Pacific Rim Riesling 1996,
> Santa Cruz, California

WALNUT/ROQUEFORT SALAD

2 heads of romaine lettuce

8-12 ounce roquefort cheese

1 cup of walnut pieces

1 cup of raisins

vinaigrette dressing of choice

Chop the lettuce, add the rest, toss and serve! People have actually asked me for this recipe but it is just four ingredients. My measurements are arbitrary. Determine amounts by appearance, just throw in handfuls of what is needed. I vary the dressing, but prefer champagne or tarragon vinegar with walnut oil.

BERRY TRIFLE

This recipe requires a deep clear glass bowl as its appeal is visual as well as flavorful.

1 pound cake (recipe follows)

2 pints each of strawberries, blueberries, and raspberries

1 quart whipping cream

2 cups cream sherry

For the pound cake:

4 cups cake flour

4 teaspoons baking powder

1 teaspoon salt

1 1/2 cups butter, cut into small pieces

8 eggs

1 cup milk

2 teaspoons vanilla extract

Sift together dry ingredients. Set aside. In a large mixing bowl, cream butter and sugar until smooth. Beat eggs in, one at a time. Add the flour mixture, alternately with the milk and vanilla. Bake in greased pans for 20 minutes in a 325ºF oven. The cake can be prepared days in advance, trifle was originally developed as a means of using up leftover cake. The day of the party, break the cake into large pieces, layer the bottom of the glass bowl. Pour a little sherry over it.

Slice the strawberries, layer some of them over the cake, so that they form a visible red line around the circumfrence of the bowl. Mix the whipped cream, sweetening to taste. (I add raw sugar). Smooth a layer of whipped cream over the strawberries, cover with a new layering of cake and sherry, layering the blueberries. Repeat the process with raspberries, and alternate until the bowl is filled. Top with whipped cream, decorate with a few berries. This dessert is very rich. A little goes a very long way; these proportions could serve twenty!

"There is no such thing as creative except by the individual."

1867	b. Spring Green, Wisconsin, father a preacher/musician, mother a teacher.
1873	Educated with the Friedrich Froebel Kindergarten system.
1885	Studied engineering at the University of Wisconsin, Madison, WI.
1888	Worked for architect Louis Sullivan, Chicago, IL.
1890	"Frank Lloyd Wright Home and Studio," Oak Park, IL.
1893	"Winslow Home," Oak Park, IL. Opened his architectural office.
1896	"Romeo and Juliet Tower," Taliesin, WI.
1904	"Larkin Office Building," Buffalo, NY.
1906	Traveled to Japan, began collection of oriental art.
1908	"Unity Temple," Oak Park, IL.
1909	"Robie House," Chicago, IL; "Coonley House," Riverside, IL. Traveled to Berlin to produce Ausgeührte Bauten Und Entwerfe (Executed Buildings and Drawings). Lived in Fiesole, Italy.
1913	"Midway Gardens," Chicago, IL' Began "Taliesin East," his studio and residence in Spring Green, WI.
1918	"Imperial Hotel," Tokyo, Japan; "Hollyhock House," Los Angeles, CA.
1923	"MIllard House," Pasadena, CA; "Charles Ennis House," Los Angeles, CA.
1927	"Arizona Biltmore Hotel," Phoenix, AZ.
1932	AN AUTOBIOGRAPHY by Frank Lloyd Wright (University of Chicago Press, Chicago).
1933	"Broadacre City," visionary project, Taliesin Fellowship.
1936	"Kaufmann House, (Falling Water)," Bear Run, PA. Began "Taliesin West," Scottsdale, AZ; "Johnson Wax Complex," Racine, WI.
1938	"Pfeiffer Chapel," Florida Southern College, Lakeland, FL.
1940	"Clarence Sondern Residence," Kansas City, MO.
1945	WHEN DEMOCRACY BUILDS by Frank Lloyd Wright (University of Chicago Press, Chicago).
1952	"Price Tower," Bartlesville, OK. "David Wright House," Phoenix, AZ.
1954	Lived in "Plaza Hotel Suite," NYC; "Sholom Synagogue," Elkins Park, PA; "Heritage - Henredon Furniture."
1956	"The Mile High Skyscraper," Chicago, IL; "Solomon Guggenheim Museum," NYC.
1958	"Marin County Civic Center," San Raphael, CA; "Gammage Auditorium," Arizona State University, Tempe, AZ.
1959	d. Scottsdale, Arizona.

PREVIOUS TWO PAGES: "TALIESIN BREAKFAST" OF IRISH OATMEAL, GRAHAM TOAST, SMOKED BACON, BAKED EGGS, FRESH SAUTEED ASPARAGUS, STRAWBERRIES, COFFEE AND AN ASSORTMENT OF FRUIT JAMS ON "CABARET" DINNERWARE FOR THE IMPERIAL HOTEL OF TOKYO, JAPAN. COMMISSIONED 1913. CHINA AND GLASSWARE BY TIFFANY & CO., COPYRIGHTED DESIGNS OWNED BY THE FRANK LLOYD WRIGHT FOUNDATION

BLACKBERRY JAM
makes about 4 - 1/2 pint jars

4 cups blackberry pulp
(with or without seeds)

3 cups sugar

1 tablespoon fresh lemon juice

Bring blackberry pulp to a boil in a large heavy kettle. Boil for 15 minutes, add sugar, continue boiling rapidly for about 45 minutes or until mixture forms thick jellied drops that stick to the edge of spoon. Add lemon juice, cool slightly, stir, pour into hot sterilized jars, seal or freeze.

APRICOT JAM
makes about 5 - 1/2 pint jars

3 packages (12 oz.) dried apricots

7 cups sugar

1 tablespoon fresh lemon juice

Cover apricots with water and soak overnight. Next day, add salt and bring to a boil for 15 minutes. Add sugar and cook until clear and desired thickness (approximately 30 minutes). Add lemon juice. Pour into hot sterilized jars and seal.

STRAWBERRY JAM
makes about 5 - 1/2 pint jars

7 cups fresh strawberries, cleaned, stemmed and sliced

3 cups sugar

1/2 tablespoon fresh lemon juice

Mash strawberries in a large heavy kettle. Cook over moderate heat until thickened. Slowly add sugar, stirring constantly over low heat until sugar is desolved.

Boil rapidly for 15 to 20 minutes until mixture sheets from your spoon. Stir occasionally, skim and pour into hot sterilized jars and seal.

PEACH JAM
makes about 3 - 1/2 pint jars

4 cups fresh peach pulp

3 cups sugar

1 tablespoon fresh lemon juice

Bring peach pulp to a boil in a large heavy kettle. Simmer until thick and clear, stirring occasionally (about 30 minutes). Pour into hot sterilized jars and seal.

THE "SOLOMON GUGGENHEIM MUSEUM," NEW YORK CITY

p10 DAVID BURKE: Quote from interview, Aspen, CO, 1996. Food photographed at James at the Mill Restaurant on 1914 Louis Vuitton Trunk. Humpty Dumpty and Brass Monkey compliments of David Burke and the Park Avenue Cafe. Recipes from: COOKING WITH DAVID BURKE (by David Burke and Carmel Berman Reingold, Alfred A. Knof, NY, 1995), permission Burke.

p14 SERGIO BUSTAMANTE: Quote from interview 1996, Food photographed at the Inn at the Mill, Johnson, AR. Recipes by Bustamante. Mirror and Jewelry, collection of the author.

p18 ALEXANDER CALDER: Quote and food preference from interview, Dallas 1971. Recipes by Miles James. Food photographed with mobile from the Fine Arts Gallery Collection, University of Arkansas, with the kind assistance of Professor Jackie Golden. The "Letter" (p18) courtesy of the Edward Durell Stone Papers, Special Collections Division, University of Arkansas Libraries, Fayetteville, AR. Thank you to Michael J. Dabrishus and Georgia Kunze. Black symbols (pp20-21) original painting from the collection of the author.

p22 CHRISTO/JEANNE CLAUDE: Quote from REICHSTAG, BERLIN, 1971-1995 (by Christo and Jeanne Claude, Taschen, Cologne, 1995). Food photographed on 18th floor balcony, the Atlantis, Miami, with Alvar Aalto vase and "Surrounded Islands Photograph" copyrighted © by Christo and photographer Wolfgang Voltz. Recipe from Christo and Jeanne Claude.

p26 SALVADOR DALI: Quote food preference from interview, New York City, 1962. Food photographed on "Easter Christ," sterling silver plate© 1972 by the Lincoln MInt. Recipe by Miles James.

p30 DEAN FEARING: Quote and recipes from DEAN FEARING'S SOUTHWEST CUISINE: BLENDING ASIA AND THE AMERICAS (Grove Weidenfeld Press, IWC, NYC, 1990) permission Fearing. Food photographed at the James at the MIll Restaurant, Johnson, AR.

GRILLED BARBEQUED GLAZED QUAIL WITH TORTILLA SALAD AND ROAST CORN-MOLASSES VINAIGRETTE

Serves 4

4 5-oz. boneless quail, wings removed
1/4 cup Mansion Barbeque Spice Mix (recipe follows)
8 slices pickled jalapeño chili
1/4 Mansion Barbecue Sauce (recipe follows)
Tortilla Salad (recipe follows)
Roast Corn-Molasses Vinaigrette (recipe follows)
4 large sprigs fresh cilantro (coriander)

Preheat grill, making sure grates are clean and rubbed or brushed with oil. sprinkle quail with Mansion Barbecue Spice Mix, making sure to coat the whole bird. Place 2 slices of pickled jalapeño chili in each quail cavity. Grill quail, breast side down, for 4 minutes. Turn quail and brush with Mansion Barbecue Sauce, coating the whole side. Grill for 3 to 4 minutes or until done. Remove quail from grill and place on cutting board to rest for 4 to 5 minutes.
Place a mound or Tortilla Salad at the "12 o'clock" position on each of four large salad plates. Ladle Roast Corn-Molasses Vinaigrette to the front of the Tortilla Salad at the "6 o'clock" position on each plate. Cut each quail in half lengthwise. Place quail with the breast toward the "6 o'clock" position and legs crisscrossed coming down off the Tortilla Salad. Place a sprig of cilantro by each quail and serve immediately.

For Mansion Barbecue Spice Mix:
2 tablespoons paprika
1 tablespoon chili powder
1 teaspoon ground cinnamon
1 teaspoon ground coriander
1 teaspoon sugar
1 teaspoon salt
1/2 teaspoon dry mustard
1/2 teaspoon black pepper
1/2 teaspoon dried thyme leaves
1/2 teaspoon curry powder
1/2 teaspoon cayenne pepper

Mix all ingredients together and store in a cool, dry place.

Mansion Barbecue Sauce:
1 tablespoon bacon fat (or vegetable oil)
1 large yellow onion, peeled and cut into 1/4-inch dice
1 cup ketchup
4 tablespoons Worcestershire sauce
1 tablespoon malt vinegar
2 tablespoons molasses
2 tablespoons Creole mustard
1 teaspoon Tabasco sauce
salt to taste
fresh lemon juice to taste
Meat drippings from smoker to taste (optional)

Preheat oven to 375º F. Heat bacon fat in a small sauté pan over medium-high heat. When hot, add onion and cook for 4 minutes or until soft. Place onion in a small ovenproof pan. Combine remaining ingredients in a small bowl and pour over onion. Cover and bake in preheated oven for 30 minutes. Remove pan from oven and keep warm until ready to serve.

For Tortilla Salad:
8 corn tortillas
8 blue corn tortillas*
8 ancho corn tortillas*
5 cups corn oil
1/2 cup black beans, cooked and drained
1/2 cup jicama, cut in 1/4-inch dice
1/2 cup red bell pepper, cut in 1/4-inch dice
1/2 cup yellow bell pepper, cut in 1/4-inch dice
3 tablespoons corn oil
1 1/2 tablespoons fresh lime juice or to taste
1 tablespoon fresh cilantro (coriander), chopped fine
2 serrano chiles, seeded and finely chopped
salt to taste

Make 3 tortilla stacks and cut each stack in half. Restack tortillas, forming 3 half-moon stacks. Starting at one end of each tortilla stack, cut 1/8-inch threads across the half moon. With the tips of your fingers, separate each piece. Combine all three colors of tortillas into one big pile. Heat 5 cups corn oil to 325ºF on a food thermometer in a medium deep-sided stockpot or deep fryer. When hot, add one-third of the tortillas. Stirring constantly, fry for 35 seconds or until crisp. Do not overcook or tortillas will lose their color and burn. Remove from oil and place tortillas on paper towel to drain. Repeat process for remaining tortillas. Reserve. In a large bowl, combine beans, jicama, bell pepper, 3 tablespoons corn oil, lime juice, cilantro, chilies, and salt and toss to mix. Adjust seasoning. Gently toss in reserved tortilla threads, being careful not to break but making sure they are well coated with dressing. Serve immediately. * Use ordinary corn tortillas if others are unobtainable.

For Roast Corn-Molasses Vinaigrette:
2 large ears sweet corn
1 tablespoon corn oil
1 medium onion, peeled and cut into 1/4-inch dice
2 cloves garlic, peeled and chopped
2 teaspoons fresh thyme, chopped
1 teaspoon cracked black pepper
1/2 cup veal demi-glace (or beef stock)
1/4 cup chicken stock
1/3 cup molasses
2 tablespoons balsamic vinegar
1 tablespoon cider vinegar
1 tablespoon Kentucky bourbon
salt to taste

Preheat oven to 450ºF. Leave corn in husks, dip in water, and place in preheated oven. Bake for 15 minutes. Remove from oven and let cool. Shuck and clean silk from corn. With a sharp knife, remove kernels. Using the dull side of the knife, scrape the cobs for pulp. Combine kernels and pulp and reserve. Heat oil in a medium saucepan over medium heat. When hot, add onion. Sauté for 4 minutes, stirring constantly. Add garlic and sauté for 1 minute. Add thyme, pepper, demi-glace or beef stock, and chicken stock. Bring to a boil. Lower heat and simmer for 5 to 7 minutes, until reduced by one-third or until slightly thickened. Heat a small saucepan over high heat. When hot, slowly pour in molasses. Allow the molasses to bubble for 3 minutes, shaking the pan constantly. Do not allow molasses to burn. Add vinegars and bourbon and cook for 3 to 4 minutes or until slightly reduced. Stir molasses mixture into demi-glace mixture and return to a boil. Immediately add reserved corn and stir to combine. If vinaigrette does not coat back of a spoon, lower heat and simmer until it reaches the proper consistency. Season with salt and keep warm.

p34 NORMAN FOSTER: Quote and food preference from interview at the American Institute of Architects "Gold Medal" ceremony, The Biltmore Hotel, L.A., CA. 1994. Food photographed in Hong Kong from the 25th floor of the Ritz Carlton Hotel. Recipe from Miles James.

p38 LINCOLN FOX: Quote from interview, 1997. Food photographed in the springs of Bella Vista Trout Farm with 4 foot bronze "The Duck Catcher." Recipe from Lincoln and Rachelle Fox.

p42 MICHAEL GRAVES: Quote and food preference from interview at the United States Ambassador's Residence, Rome, Italy, 1994. Food photographed on 7th floor balcony of the Swan/Westin Hotel, Walt Disney World, Orlando, FL. Recipes by Miles James.

p46 NANCY GRAVES: Quote from interview, the American Academy in Rome, Rome, Italy, 1980. Food photographed at James at the Mill Restaurant, Johnson, AR. Recipes from Nancy Graves.

p50 LOIS GREENFIELD: Quote from BREAKING BOUNDS, THE DANCE PHOTOGRAPHY OF LOIS GREENFIELD (Thames and Hudson, UK and Chronicle Books, USA, 1992). Food photographed at James at the Mill Restaurant, Johnson, AR. Swedish Pancake recipe by MIles James; Crusted Swordfish recipe by Dereck Brewley and Michael Caracciolo.

p54 RICHARD HAAS: Quote from interview 1995. Food photographed by "Cascades" mural, The Bakery Center, Miami, FL, 1996. The mural was demolished the following week. Recipes from Richard Haas and Katherine Sokolindoff Haas (borscht by Miles James).

p58 KEITH HARING: Quote from KEITH HARING (by Elizabeth Sussman, Whitney/Bulfinch Press, NYC, 1997). Food photographed on "Best Buddies"© Keith Haring Foundation, by permission 1997. Food preference from interview in Saks Fifth Avenue, NYC, 1987. Recipes by Miles James.

p62 WILLIAM HARPER: Quote from interview at the Orlando Museum of Art, Orlando, 1990. Food photographed with cloisonné lapel pin (with Courtney's baby tooth) at James at the Mill Restaurant, Johnson, AR. Recipes by William, Riva and Josh Harper.

p66 ROBERT HEINDEL: Quote from interview, 1995. Food photographed at James at the Mill Restaurant, Johnson, AR, on "Imperial" Frank Lloyd Wright dinnerware by Tiffany and Company. Recipe by Robert and Rose Heindel.

p70 ALLAN HOUSER: Quote and food preference from interview, Santa Fe, NM, 1991. Food photographed on Lakota 1890 beaded vest at James at the Mill Restaurant, Johnson, AR. Recipes by Miles James.

p74 MILES JAMES: Quote and recipes by Miles James. Food photographed at James at the Mill Restaurant and Inn at the Mill, Johnson, AR.

WARM GOAT CHEESE SALAD WITH YUKON GOLD POTATOES AND FRISSE

Serves 4-6

10 ounces heavy cream
5 ounces fresh goat cheese
2 tablespoons fresh chopped thyme leaves
1 fresh shallot, minced
1 ounce corn oil, for sauteing
1 head baby frisse
8 strips smoked bacon, small dice, reserve fat
4 Yukon Gold potatoes
1 fresh bunch Italian parsley
2 ounces chili powder, medium to dark color
Balsamic vinegar, good quality
1 fresh Granny Smith apple
extra corn oil for the infused oil
1 tablespoon each fresh parsley, chive, tarragon, thyme for chopping

For the goat cheese fondue:
In a heavy bottom non-reactive sauce pan sweat the minced shallot in the hot corn oil until translucent. Stir in the fresh chopped thyme, add the cream and bring to a boil. Turn the heat off and immediately stir in the goat cheese. Continue to stir using a whisk until the goat cheese is incorporated, season to taste with salt and fresh cracked black pepper. You can reserve the fondue in a steam bath for up to two hours. You want the sauce to be a nice thin consistency. Thin with hot cream if needed when plating the salad.

For the Yukon Gold potatoes:
Trim the potatoes into a rectangle shape leaving as much height to the potato as possible. Dice the trim into small uniform pieces and reserve. Deep fry the rectangle pieces (370ºF) and the small dice separately until golden brown. The rectangle pieces will need to be finished in a 375ºF oven until cooked through. Season both with salt, fresh cracked black pepper as soon as they come out of the fryer, and reserve at room temperature until service.

For the parsley and chili oil and balsamic reduction:
Take the bunch of parsley and rough chop. Place the parsley in a blender with enough corn oil to cover and mix on high for three minutes. After the parsley is mixed strain through a chinois and put in a squirt-bottle. For the chili oil place the ground chili powder in a heavy bottomed non-reactive sauce pan and lightly toast until you can smell the chili powder. Cover the chili powder with 6 ounces of corn oil and bring to a boil. After the oil boils turn the heat off and let steep for thirty minutes, then strain through a chinois and place in a squirt bottle.

For the salad:
Render the small diced smoked bacon and reserve the fat. In a mixing bowl, mix equal parts of the reserved bacon fat with a good quality balsmaic vinegar, season with salt and pepper. Toss the cleaned frisse with the rendered bacon bits, warm diced Yukon gold potato, and fresh chopped herbs, (parsley, chive, tarragon, thyme), with the bacon balsamic vinaigrette. Place the salad in the back of a warm salad plate. Stand the warm rectangle in the center of the plate and using a parring knife cut a small hole in the top so that you can only see the hole from the top. Ladle 2 ounces of the warm goat cheese fondue in front of the rectangle and salad and to the sides. Cut one side of the Granny Smith apple off and slice it into thin long slices. Insert four slices, arranged into a fan, into the small hole in the top of the rectangle. Garnish the goat cheese fondue with parsley and chili oil and balsamic reduction.

GRILLED CORN MUSH WITH SPAGHETTI SQUASH, SHIITAKE MUSHROOMS, SUN-DRIED TOMATOES AND PEA BASIL COULIS

Serves 4-6

2 cups chicken stock
1 cup corn meal
2 tablespoons roast garlic purée
1 cup grated parmesan
1/2 cup roasted corn kernels
1 tablespoon fresh chopped parsley
1 tablespoon fresh chopped chives
salt and fresh ground black pepper

For the corn mush:

In a heavy bottom sauce pot bring the chicken stock to a boil. Whisk in the corn meal, reduce the heat to a simmer. Season with salt and pepper to taste. Add the roast garlic purée, roast corn kernels and fresh chopped herbs. Fold in the parmesan cheese and check the seasoning. Once the corn mush is cooked spread onto a greased cookie sheet to a thickness of about 2 inches. wrap with plastic wrap and refrigerate. Once the corn mush cools, unwrap and cut out disks using a cookie or biscuit cutter. Reserve cold until later.

For the vegetables and coulis:
medium spaghetti squash
1 medium white onion, small dice
1 tablespoon fresh chopped garlic
8 ounces fresh shiitake mushrooms, remove stem and quarter
4 ounces sundried tomatoes, sliced
4 ounces green peas
1 tablespoon champagne vinegar
1 tablespoon fresh chopped parsley
1 tablespoon fresh chopped chives
1 ounce fresh basil leaves
olive oil
salt and fresh ground black pepper

Split the spaghetti squash and discard seeds. Steam the spaghetti squash until tender. Using a fork remove the meat of the squash from the shell. Cool and reserve.

For the mushrooms:
In a heavy bottom sauté pan, sauté the white onion in a tablespoon each of olive oil and butter. Once onions are trasnlucent, add the garlic and sauté until golden brown. Add the shiitakes, season with salt and pepper and sauté until tender. Fold in the sundried tomatoes and reserve them.

For the pea basil coulis:
In a blender purée the green peas, champagne vinegar, and basil. Add olive oil to sauce consistency and season with salt and pepper. Pass through a fine mesh strainer and reserve.

To assemble:
Grill the corn mush disks until hot throughout. Reheat your spaghetti squash in a heavy bottom sauté pan with a little olive oil, season with salt and pepper. On a plate using a metal ring mold, divide the spaghetti squash into the ring molds and press down firmly with the back of a spoon. Next layer the shiitake mushroom mixture into the ring molds and press down with the back of a spoon. Remove the ring molds and place the hot corn mush disks on top of the vegetables. Garnish the plate with the pea basil coulis.

WARM CHOCOLATE CAKE WITH CARAMEL ICE CREAM AND CHOCOLATE SPIRAL COOKIE

For the chocolate cake:
3 eggs
3/4 cup sugar
6 ounces semisweet chocolate
3 ounces butter
1/4 cup water

In a bowl, mix eggs and 1/4 cup of the sugar to light consistency. Combine water and other 1/2 cup sugar in a small heavy bottom sauce pat. Heat until sugar dissolves in water, forming simple syrup. Remove from heat. Add butter and chocolate and stir until incorporated. Fold the butter and chocolate mixture into the egg mixture. Ladle 2 ounces of cake batter into individual greased "non-stick" molds* and bake at 400ºF for 10 minutes. Serve with caramel ice cream and chocolate spiral cookies.

For the ice cream:
2 cups sugar
1/2 cup water
15 egg yolks
1 quart heavy whipping cream
1/2 quart whole milk

Combine one cup of the sugar and the water in a heavy bottom sauce pot. Cook on medium heat until mixture starts to caramelize. While that is caramelizing, combine egg yolks and the other cup of sugar in a mixing bowl and whip to a white ribbon. Heat milk and cream until scalded. Once sugar has caramelized, combine with milk, then whip in egg mixture. Allow to cool. Pass through strainer and freeze.

For the spiral cookies:
12 ounces butter
8 ounces honey
20 ounces all purpose flour
24 ounces powdered sugar
4 ounces cocoa
8 ounces egg whites
(approximately 6-7 eggs)

Cream butter and honey together. Sift together dry ingredients and add half of this to the cream mixture. Add egg whites and the other half of the dry ingredients. After all of the ingredients have been added together, mix for approximately 15 minutes or until smooth and well-mixed. Spread tuille cookies onto a non-stick baking sheet into desired shape and bake at 400ºF for approximately 3 minutes.

MILK CHOCOLATE CARAMEL CREME BRULEE

For the crème brûlée:
3 cups milk
2 3/4 cups heavy cream
1 cup sugar
1/2 cup water
12 ounces milk chocolate, chopped
8 egg yolks

Combine milk, heavy cream and half of the sugar in a heavy bottom stainless steel pan and hat until scalding hot. Simultaneously combine the other half of the sugar and water in a heavy bottom stainless steel pan and heat to an amber caramelized color. Add the caramelized sugar to the cream mixture, being very careful, the cream will bubble a lot, and stir with a whisk to incorporate. Pour the caramel and cream mixture over the chopped chocolate and stir with a whisk until all the chocolate is melted and well incorporated. Next you will need to cool the chocolate mixture on an ice bath until cold. Add the egg yolks and stir to incorporate, then strain through a fine mesh strainer (chinoise tamis). This recipe can be completed up to this point 2 or 3 days in advance. *To bake the creme brulees:* Pour the creme brulee base into ceramic baking dishes of your choice (I like the classic white round or oval dish, 1-inch high), and place the baking dishes in a water bath or bain marie. Bake 45-55 minutes at 325ºF. Remove from oven and move from water bath to a resting rack for 20-30 minutes, then refrigerate. Sprinkle the top with sugar and caramelize with a blow torch. Garnish with fresh fruit and mint and cookies.

FAYE'S WARM BANANA CAKE WITH CARAMEL GLAZE

1 1/2 cups sugar
3 eggs
2 cups flour
1/2 cup buttermilk
1/4 teaspoon salt
1/2 cup butter
1 cup mashed bananas
1 teaspoon soda
1 teaspoon vanilla extract
6 ounces Karo light corn syrup
3 ounces brown sugar
1 tablespoon butter
1 ounce cream
malt ice cream
chopped pecans
fresh mint sprigs

Mix soda and buttermilk, set aside. Mix flour and salt, set aside. Cream butter and sugar until well blended. Add one egg at a time until all three are used. Add bananas. Add milk mixture alternately with flour mixture until all are blended. Add vanilla. Pour into two nine-inch cake pans that have been prepared, and bake at 350ºF for 25-30 minutes. At James at the Mill, we use a non-stick baking pan that holds about 3 ounces of batter for an individual serving. The non-stick baking pan is called a *"Wolfgang Puck" mold and can be bought at Bridge Kitchen Ware at 214 East 52nd street (between 2nd and 3rd Avenues), in New York City, NY, (212) 688-4220 or 1-800-274-3435. Ask for Steve. Test the cake with a toothpick. If it comes out clean, it is done. Turn the cake out onto a resting rack and let cool.

For the butterscotch caramel:
In a heavy bottomed non-reactive skillet, add the Karo corn syrup, brown sugar, and butter. Bring to a boil. Simmer until it is a rich golden-brown color. Add cream and bring back to a boil, transfer to a bain marie (water bath), keep warm. *To plate the dish:* Take the individual portion, or a slice of the cooled cake, and warm in a 400ºF oven. Ladle 2 ounces of the butterscotch caramel onto a warm plate. Place the banana cake in the middle of the sauce and shingle thin sliced bananas on top of the cake. Sprinkle with sugar and caramelize with a blow torch. Serve with a scoop of malt ice cream. Scoop the ice cream and toss in chopped pecans, then place on top of the caramelized banana slices. Garnish the plate with fresh mint.

INTENSE LEMON TART WITH RASPBERRY SORBET AND CHOCOLATE CRINKLE COOKIES

For the filling:
3 lemons, zest and juice
2 egg yolks
1 whole egg
2 1/2 ounces butter
3 ounces sugar

Chop the lemon zest fine. Add the lemon juice, chopped zest, butter and sugar to a heavy bottom stainless steel pan. Over medium heat, stir until butter melts and liquid comes to a boil. While liquid is coming to a boil, whisk egg and egg yolks well. Add half of the heated liquid to the whisked eggs and whisk until well incorporated. Once well incorporated, add this mixture to the other half of the heated liquid in the pan and whisk well. Whisk continuously, over medium-high heat, until the mixture has thickened and starts to boil on the sides. Remove from the heat and chill immediately.

For lemon tart shells:
1 cup flour
1/3 cup butter, cut into small pieces
1/4 cup sugar
1 lemon, zest only, finely chopped
1 egg
extra flour for dusting

Combine all ingredients into an electric mixing bowl, except for the egg. Using the dough hook, mix the ingredients until well incorporated. Add the egg and mix. Dust the sides of the bowl with the extra flour until dough pulls away from sides cleanly. Remove from the mixing bowl, wrap in plastic and chill. Once the dough is cooled and you're ready to bake the tart shells you will need a floured wooden surface, a rolling pin, and some tart shells. Roll the dough out on the floured surface until very thin, then cut circle a little bigger than your tart shells and press the circles into your prepared tart shells, (non-stick tart shells work well, otherwise use a little non-stick cooking spray and flour). Bake tart shells until golden brown at 350ºF.

RASPBERRY SORBET

23 ounces raspberries
1 ounce sugar
juice of one lemon

In a heavy bottom non-reactive sauce pot, combine all ingredients and bring to a boil. Remove from heat, puree, pass through a fine mesh strainer, cool and freeze in a batch freezer.

CHOCOLATE CRINKLE COOKIES

4 squares baking chocolate
1/2 cup vegetable oil
2 cups sugar
4 eggs
2 cps flour
2 tablespoons baking powder
1/2 teaspoon salt
1 cup powder sugar, to roll cookies in before baking

Melt the baking chocolate and vegetable oil in a heavy bottom stainless steel pan. Add the chocolate and oil mixture to an electric mixing bowl. Mix in the sugar and whip until shiny. Add the eggs one at a time, mix until well incorporated. Add the flour, baking powder and salt, and mix until well incorporated. Remove from mixing bowl and chill overnight. The next day roll the dough into little balls and submerge in the powder sugar, then place on a non-stick baking sheet and bake at 350ºF for 3-4 minutes or to desired doneness. *To plate the dish:* Fill the tart shells with the lemon filling and place on raspberry coulis. Place the cookie close to the tart and scoop some raspberry sorbet on top. Garnish with fresh mint and powdered sugar.

p78 FAY JONES: Quote from FAY JONES (by Robert Ivey, Jr. AIA Press, Washington, DC, 1992). Food photographed at Cooper Chapel, Bella Vista, AR. Recipe by Miles James.

p82 DOUGLAS KIRKLAND: Quote from THE LIGHT YEARS (by Douglas Kirkland, Thames and Huson, Inc, NYC, 1989). Food photography at James at the Mill Restaurant, Johnson, AR. Recipes from Douglas and Françoise Kirkland. Cake by Chef Miles James.

p86 JAMES LAMBETH: Quote and recipes by James Lambeth. Food photography at the McKamey/James Residence, Fayetteville, AR, and on SUNDANCING cover image. Thank you Mom for the fried pies and recipe.

p90 ROY LICHTENSTEIN: Quote and food preference from interview at Leo Castelli Party, NYC, 1995. Food photographed with Taittinger Champagne Lichtenstein Bottle. Medal photographed at The American Academy in Rome. Recipe from Miles James.

P94 CHARLES RENNIE MACKINTOSH: Quote from CHARLES RENNIE MACKINTOSH (by Richard Drew Publishing, Glasgow Scotland, 1987). Food photographed in room #122, The Inn at the Mill, Johnson, AR. Food preference from interview with Pamela Robertson curator of Hunterian Art Gallery, University of Glasgow, Glasgow, Scotland, 1995. Recipe by Miles James.

p98 GIACOMO MANZÚ: Quote and food preference from interview at The American Academy in Rome, Italy, 1980. Food photographed at James at the Mill Restaurant, Johnson, AR, with Lincoln Fox's "Doves." Recipes by Miles James.

p102 HILTON MCCONNICO:Quote from HILTON MCCONNICO by Michel Areline, (Memphis Brooks Museum, Memphis, TN 1990). Food photographed at Lambeth Residence, Fayetteville, AR. Recipes by Hilton McConnico.

p106 RICHARD MEIER: Quote from RICHARD MEIER (Rizzoli International, NYC, 1997), Food photographed at the "High Museum of Art," in Atlanta, GA. Recipe from Richard Meier.

p110 MARK MILLER: Quote and recipes from COYOTE CAFE (by Mark Miller, Ten Speed Press, Berkely, CA, 1989). Food photographed at James at the Mill Restaurant, Johnson, AR. Permission Miller.

p114 ISAMU NOGUCHI: Quote and food preference from interview 1984. Food photographed at James Residence, Fayetteville, AR. Recipe by Miles James.

p118 BON PAINTER: Quote from his painting, "The Cros Eyed Talking Horse." Food photographed with painting in Miami, FL, floor 18, the Atlantis. Food preference from his nephew Billy Ames, Watts, OK. Recipes by Miles James.

p122 MICHAEL PARKES: Quote from MICHAEL PARKES: 1977-1992 (Steltman Editions, Amsterdam, 1993). Food photographed at James at the Mill Restaurant, Johnson, AR. Recipes by Michael and Maria Parkes.

p126 I.M. PEI: Quote form I.M. PEI (by Carter Wiseman, Harry N. Abrams, Inc. Publishers, NY, 1990). Food photographed in Hong Kong from the 25th floor of the Ritz Carlton Hotel on Rangthong stainless steel plates. Recipe by Miles James based on Mr. Pei's love of orange juice.

p130 CESAR PELLI: Quote from CESAR PELLI: SELECTED AND CURRENT WORKS (Images Publishing, Australia, 1993). Food photographed at James at the Mill Restaurant, Johnson, AR, with original drawing of Herring Hall. Recipe from Cesar Pelli.

p134 ELSA PERETTI: Quote from Tiffany and Company. Food photographed on "Silver Soup Tureen with Padova Ladle and Crystal Thumbprint Bowls," at Savoy Waterfall in Wedington, AR. Recipe by Elsa Peretti.

p138 ANTOINE PREDOCK: Quote from ANTOINE PREDOCK: ARCHITECT (Rizzoli International Publications, NY, 1994). Food photographed at the "Las Vegas Central Library and Children's Discovery Museum," Las Vegas, NV. Food was provided by Ken Rissolo in the Coyote Restaurant at the MGM Grand Hotel. Recipe courtesy of the Shed Restaurant, Santa Fe, NM.

p142 EMILIO PUCCI: Quote from PUCCI: A RENAISSANCE IN FASHION (by Shirley Kennedy, Abberville Press, NY, London Press, Paris, 1991). Food photographed on Joyce's Pucci Dress. Food preference from interview in Florence, Italy, at the Pucci Palace, 1985. Recipe by Courtney James.

p146 WOLFGANG PUCK/BARBARA LAZAROFF: Quote (Puck) and recipes from WOLFGANG PUCK: ADVENTURES IN THE KITCHEN (by Wolfgang Puck Random House, NY, 1991), permission Puck. Quote (Lazaroff), RESTAURANTS THAT WORK, (by Martin E. Dorf, Whitney Library of Design, NY, 1992). Food photographed at James at the Mill Restaurant, Johnson, AR.

CONTINUED FROM PAGE 149 To prepare the sauce, heat 1 tablespoon peanut oil in a 10-inch skillet. Over medium heat, sauté the mushrooms for 2 to 3 minutes. Deglaze the pan with the red and plum wines and reduce to a glaze. Pour in the brown stock and reduce until the sauce thickens. Whisk in the butter and season with salt and pepper to taste. Keep warm. Just before serving, stir in the garlic, green onion, ginger, and chili flakes. Correct seasoning to taste. Meanwhile, butterfly the squab and remove all but the leg bones. Season lightly with salt and pepper. Grill, skin-side down, about 5 minutes, turn and grill 5 minutes longer. Finish skin-side down just to crisp. (To sauté, heat 1 tablespoon peanut oil in an ovenproof skillet. Brown both sides quickly and transfer to the oven. Roast 10 to 12 minutes, or until medium rare.) To prepare the watercress, heat the remaining 1 tablespoon peanut oil in a small skillet. Sauté the watercress for 1 to 2 minutes, just to wilt. Stir in the rice wine vinegar and the remaining 1 teaspoon sesame oil and season with salt and pepper to taste. Separate the breasts, legs and wings. Cut each breast into 4 slices. Reheat the pancake and cut into quarters. For presentation, mound the watercress in the center of a large platter. Arrange the noodles around the salad, points facing in, leaving a little space between each quarter. Place 2 slices of breast on each quarter and alternate the legs and wings around the noodles. Spoon the sauce over the squab and the noodles. Serve immediately.

For Chili Pasta Dough:
1 1/2 cups all-purpose flour
1 1/2 cups semolina flour
1 teaspoon salt
4 large eggs
2 to 3 tablespoons chile oil

In a food processor fitted with the steel blade, combine the flours, salt, eggs, and 2 tablespoons of oil, adding the third if needed. Process just until the dough holds together when pinched. Turn out onto a very lightly floured surface and knead into a ball. Wrap in plastic wrap and let rest at room temperature at least 30 minutes.When ready to roll out the dough, cut into 4 pieces and roll and cut as desired, keeping the unused dough covered to prevent drying out.

PEACH AND BERRY COBBLER
Serves 12

1 recipe shortcake (recipe follows)
heavy cream
sugar

For the Filling:
3 pounds (8 or 9) ripe peaches
4 cups (2 baskets) blackberries,
blueberries, raspberries,
or a combination
3 tablespoons dark brown sugar
3 tablespoons all-purpose flour
3 tablespoons lemon juice
2 tablespoons peach brandy, kirsch, or
Grand Marnier
1/2 teaspoon cinnamon
pinch of freshly grated nutmeg
1/3 cup streusel (recipe follows)

Preheat the oven to 375° F. Line one or two baking trays with parchment paper. Prepare the shortcake dough, and roll out to 1/2-inch thickness. Cut out 12 2 1/2-inch circles, rerolling the dough as necessary. Arrange the circles on the prepared trays, brush the tops with cream, and sprinkle lightly with sugar. Bake 5 minutes, reduce the oven temperature to 350° F and continue baking 15 to 20 minutes longer, until just lightly golden. Blanch the peaches, peel, cut in half, and remove the pits. Cut each half into 4 slices and place in a large bowl. Combine with the remaining ingredients, tossing well. Let sit 20 to 30 minutes. Raise the oven temperature to 375° F. Lightly butter an 8 1/2 x 13 1/2 x 2 1/2-inch baking dish. Spoon the fruit into the dish, spreading it evenly. Sprinkle the streusel over and arrange the shortcakes on top (4 each across three rows). Bake 40 minutes, until the shortcakes are nicely browned. Serve warm with your favorite ice cream, softly whipped cream, or just as it is with a sprinkling of sifted powdered sugar.

For Shortcake:
2 3/4 cups pastry or cake flour
1/4 cup sugar
1 tablespoon plus
1 teaspoon baking powder
1 teaspoon salt
10 tablespoons (5 ounces) chilled
unsalted butter,
cut into 1-ounce pieces
1 cup heavy cream

In a food processor fitted with the steel blade, combine the flour, sugar, baking powder, and salt with a few on/off turns. Add the chilled butter and process just until combined. With the motor running, pour the cream through the feed tube, stopping just before the dough forms a ball. Turn out the dough onto a lightly floured surface and gently knead, forming a smooth ball. Do not overwork.

For Struesel:
1/4 cup (2 ounces)
unblanched whole almonds
1/3 cup pastry flour
2 tablespoons brown sugar
2 tablespoons white sugar
1 1/2 teaspoons ground cinnamon
3/4 teaspoon freshly
grated nutmeg
pinch of ground cardamom
4 tablespoons (2 ounces) unsalted
butter, chilled and cut
into small pieces
1/3 cup quick oats

Preheat oven to 350° F. Arrange almonds on a baking tray and toast 15 to 18 minutes, turning occasionally with a spatula. Cool. Chop coarsely and set aside. In a food processor fitted with the steel blade, combine the flour, the sugars, cinnamon, nutmeg, and cardamom with on/of turns. Add the butter and process just until the mixture comes together. Transfer to a small bowl and stir in the oats and almonds. Refrigerate, covered, until needed.

p150 JAIVID RANGTHONG: Quote from THAI HOME INDUSTRIES Publication. Food photographed at the Oriental Hotel, Bangkok. Silver headdress from the Golden Triangle, Inc. Bangkok. Recipes from the Rangthong Family. Drawings by Haiti Rangthong.

p154 FREDERIC REMINGTON: Quote and food preference from FREDERIC REMINGTON: THE MASTERWORKS (by Michael Edward Shapiro and Peter H. Hassrick, essays by David McCullough, Doreen Bolger Burke, and John Seelye, Abradale Press, Harry N. Abrams, NY, 1991). Food photographed in room #222 at the Inn at the Mill, Johnson, AR. Recipes by Miles James.

p158 ZANDRA RHODES: Quote from THE ART OF ZANDRA RHODES (by Zandra Rhodes, Jonathan Cape, Ltd., London, 1984). Food photographed with Zandra's dress design for Joyce Lambeth for Courtney and Miles' wedding, Miami, FL, 1994. Recipes by Zandra Rhodes.

ZANDRA'S SPECIAL FLORAL SALAD

Use any fabulous, edible greenery available - clean, rinse and mix loosely in an artistic bowl. You can use some or all of the following ingredients:

Onion flowers;
Nasturtium flowers;
Purple and green lettuce leaves;
Lovage leaves;
Borage flowers;
Pine nuts.

For the Dressing:
juice of 2 lemons
(approximately 2 tablespoons)
peppercorns (freshly ground by
hammering in a pestle and mortar)
1 teaspoon powdered
English mustard
salt
aniseed
fennel seeds
2 teaspoons sugar
sesame seed salt
4 tablespoons olive oil

Dissolve sugar and mustard in the lemon juice. Add burnt sesame seed salt and pepper and whisk until there are no lumps in the mustard and the sugar dissolves. Add salt, aniseed and fennel seeds. Add olive oil, (double the amount of lemon juice, approx. 4 tablespoons). Transfer mixture to a jar with a tightly fitted lid. Shake well. Toss with salad mixture before serving. Sprinkle with sesame salt, and scatter fresh nasturtium flowers.

p164 RICHARD ROGERS: Quote from RICHARD ROGERS: 1978-1988 (A+U Publishing, Tokyo, 1988). Food photographed in Lambeth Residence, Fayetteville, AR. Recipes by Miles James who prepared the dinner for Richard Rogers and his staff in the Rogers' residence, Chelsea, London, 1993.

p168 JAMES ROSENQUIST: Quote from interview at Aripeka, FL. Food photographed with art from the collection of the author. Recipe for Stone Crab Claw Pasta from Sweets Famous Fish Restaurant at Southstreet in Manhattan, NY. Grape salad recipe by Wolfgang Puck, remaining recipes by Miles James.

BOLOGNESE PASTA
serves 4

1/4 cup butter
3 tablespoons olive oil
1 cup fresh basil
10-15 Greek olives
1 medium onion chopped finely
1 medium carrot chopped finely
1 medium celery stalk
chopped finely
1/4 pound pancetta or bacon
chopped finely
1 1/2 pounds ground beef
salt and pepper to taste
2 cups red wine
(or a shot of brandy)
3-4 fresh tomatoes,
skinned and seeded
1/2 cup milk

Heat butter and oil in a large sauce pan until butter foams. Add onion, carrot, celery and pancetta (or bacon). Sautè over meduim heat until browning begins. Add meat and cook and stir until meat turns brown. Increase heat and add wine. Stir tomatoes into meat mixutre. Cover and reduce heat and simmer (1 to 1 1/2 hours) until sauce thickens to desired consistancy. Stir occasionally. Add milk and simmer 5 minutes longer. Mix with 1 pound prepared spaghetti pasta. Top with grated parmesan cheese. *One tablespoon of aniseed may be substituted for meat in this recipe.*

p172 FRITZ SCHOLDER: Quote from FRITZ SCHOLDER (Rizzoli, NY, 1982). Food photographed at Bunky Boger Buffalo Ranch, Lowell, AR, on Nambi Ware. Recipes by Fritz Scholder.

p178 BOŘEK ŠÍPEK: Quote from BOŘEK ŠÍPEK (Steltman Editions, Amsterdam, 1995). Food photographed with "Odette" Chalice from Luminaire of Coral Gables, FL. Recipes by Bořek Šípek.

p182 LAURINDA SPEAR: Quote from ARQUITECTRONICA (AIA Press, Wash., DC, 1991). Food photographed in Miami at the "Spear House" (Thank you Fredric and Katherine Mann), and in the "Sky Court" of the "Atlantis." Recipes from Laurinda Spear.

p188 PHILIPPE STARCK: Quote from interview. A special thank you to Ms Sian Griffiths of the Peninsula Hotel, Hong Kong, for her inside tour of FELIX RESTAURANT and the "Glass Objects" by Philippe Starck commemorating the tower opening in 1994. Recipes and drawings by Philippe Starck.

p194 EDWARD DURELL STONE: Quote from interview at the Fine Arts Gallery, University of Arkansas, Fayetteville, AR, 1970. Food photographed at the "Married Student Housing," University of Arkansas, Fayetteville, AR. "Blini" and "Spoon Bread" recipes from Maria Stone (compliments of the Edward Durell Stone Papers, Special Collections Division, University of Arkansas, Fayetteville, AR. Additional recipes by Miles James.

p198 ERNEST TROVA: Quote from TROVA (by Kultermann and Kagan, Abrams, NY, 1987). Food photographed in the Lambeth Residence Gallery, with art from the collection of the author. Recipe by Carla and Ernest Trova.

p202 ROBERT VENTURI: Quote from COMPLEXITY AND CONTRADICTION IN ARCHITECTURE (by Robert Venturi, Museum of Modern Art, NYC, 1966). Food photographed on his "Flower" dinnerware for Swid Powell at James at the Mill Restaurant, Johnson, AR. Food preference from correspondence. Recipes by Miles James.

p206 MASSIMO VIGNELLI: Quote from DESIGN: VIGNELLI, (Rizzoli International Publications, Inc. 1990). Food photographed on 18th floor of "The Atlantis," Miami, FL, in his "Colorstone" dinnerware for Saski and his "Metafloral" coffee table. Thank you Mitzi and John Delap for use of your "Max Stacking Dinnerware" for Heller. Recipe by Massimo Vignelli.

p210 ANDY WARHOL: Quote from THE PHILOSOPHY OF ANDY WARHOL: FROM A TO B AND BACK AGAIN (Jovanovich Press, NY, 1975). Food photography of "Flower"© Andy Warhol Foundation, by permission 1997 at the Inn at the Mill, Johnson, AR, from the collection of the author. Food preference from an interview at Saks Fifth Avenue, NY, 1987. Recipes by Miles James.

p214 BJØRN WIINBLAD: Quote and food preference from interview, Dallas, TX, 1994. Food photographed at Lambeth Residence, Fayetteville, AR. Recipe by Miles James.

p218 JAMES WINES/KRIZ KIZAK: Quote (Wines) from DE-ARCHITECTURE (by James Wines, Rizzoli, NY, 1987). Quote (Kizak) from correspondence. Food photographed at James at the Mill Restaurant, Johnson, AR. Recipes from Kriz Kizak.

p222 FRANK LLOYD WRIGHT: Quote from AN AUTOBIOGRAPHY (by Frank Lloyd Wright, University of Chicago Press, Chicago, 1932). Food photographed in room #220, Inn at the Mill, Johnson, AR, on "Cabaret" dinnerware by Tiffany and Company, NY. (Thank you Linda Coy for your interest and research). Food preference from AN AUTOBIOGRAPHY. Recipes by Miles James.

PHILIPPE STARCK," PASTA"

THANKS
TO THE ARTISTS
FOR THEIR RECIPES,
THEIR PRECIOUS TIME,
THEIR HUMOR, AND
THEIR CONSTANT
INSPIRATION

THANKS MOM

(APRICOT FRIED PIES, RECIPE P89)

WILLIAM HARPER

SERGIO BUSTAMANTE

LAURINDA SPEAR

ANDY WARHOL

ELSA PERETTI

FRITZ SCHOLDER

ROBERT HEINDEL

MASSIMO VIGNELLI

JAMES ROSENQUIST

NANCY GRAVES

PHILIPPE STARCK

LOIS GREENFIELD

RICHARD HAAS

CHRISTO/JEANNE CLAUDE

ALLAN HOUSER

BJØRN WIINBLAD

ERNEST TROVA

MARK MILLER

MICHAEL GRAVES

FAY JONES

LINCOLN FOX

BOŘEK ŠÍPEK

ALEXANDER CALDER

RICHARD MEIER

CESAR PELLI

DOUGLAS KIRKLAND

MANZU

NORMAN FOSTER

MICHAEL PARKES

HILTON MCCONNICO

DEAN FEARING

ZANDRA RHODES

JAMES WINES

BON PAINTER

ROBERT VENTURI

ANTOINE PREDOCK